ACCIDENTS IN
NORTH AMERICAN
MOUNTAINEERING

1993

ACCIDENTS IN NORTH AMERICAN MOUNTAINEERING

VOLUME 6 • NUMBER 4 • ISSUE 46

1993

THE AMERICAN ALPINE CLUB
GOLDEN

THE ALPINE CLUB OF CANADA
BANFF

ISSN 0065-082X

ISBN 0-930-410-56-4

Manufactured in the United States of America

Published by
The American Alpine Club, Inc.
710 Tenth Street
Golden, CO 80401

Cover Illustration
A typical May or June day on the Kahiltna Glacier during the climbing season, when one may encounter as many as a hundred others, coming or going, on the way to the West Buttress of Mount McKinley. There is little liklihood of getting off route, but the hazards of concealed crevasses, severe weather, and altitude sickness cannot be diminished merely by an increase in human activity. Photograph by Jed Williamson.

This publication was supported in part by grants from:

The New York Section of The American Alpine Club
The Steve Gordon Memorial Fund (established in 1992)

SAFETY COMMITTEES 1993

The American Alpine Club

Dr. Benjamin G. Ferris, Jr., John Dill, Fred Stanley, Rick Wilcox, James Yester, and John E. (Jed) Williamson *(Chairman)*

The Alpine Club of Canada

Ian Findlay, Helmut Microys, Orvel Miskiw, Paul Ritzema, and Murray Toft *(Chairman)*

CONTENTS

ACCIDENTS IN
NORTH AMERICAN MOUNTAINEERING

Forty-Sixth Annual Report of the
Safety Committees of The American Alpine Club
and The Alpine Club of Canada

This is the forty-sixth issue of Accidents in North American Mountaineering and the fifteenth that has been done jointly by the American Alpine Club and The Alpine Club of Canada.

Canada: Again, happily, we have fewer mountaineering accidents to report this year than last, though a greater number than usual happened when hikers got into trouble after wandering into mountaineering terrain. Usually we do not include these, but as we have mentioned in the past, the difference is sometimes unclear, and our following reports include two borderline cases. In both, the people involved were referred to as hikers in the information we received; also, they were not equipped as typical mountaineers, so some elitists among us would dismiss them as non-mountaineers. However, labels are easy to attach and often a matter of opinion, just as the equipment required for any mountaineering project is a matter of personal choice and opinion. In view of the modern trend toward lightweight, minimal equipment and fast ascents, it seems only fair to consider the objective being undertaken in each case when deciding whether to call it a mountaineering endeavor. This includes deciding whether the individuals involved are to be called climbers.

As for the accidents reported, the causes continue to be much as they have been in the past. But we are seeing a new development in the summoning of help. The use of portable radios and cellular phones is becoming more common place. In some cases, this technology was important, if not critical, to the survival of the victims. The question has been raised, as it was when avalanche transceivers became standard equipment, as to whether the availability of such technology will result in people having a false sense of confidence and security to the extent that they go on terrain that is beyond their capability. The spectre that is raised is whether or not carrying such communication devices will ultimately be required by the custodians of our public lands, and at what cost both in terms of dollars and personal freedom.

A number of people deserve our gratitude for collecting information, andfor submitting and preparing reports this year. They include Terry Damm, Burke Duncan, George Field, G. Fortin, Denis Gravel, D. Humphrey, Terry Willis, Percy Woods, plus some who declined mention and any we have regrettably missed.

United States: This year the reader will find for the first time a full length narrative on an accident in Mexico. The volcanoes are not far from a transportation center, and Pico de Orizaba is the third highest mountain in North America. They are understandable popular destinations, especially for commercially guided trips. We know that AMS and HAPE incidents happen there with regularity, but rarely with dire results, as the routes are straight forward and evacuations do not have the technical requirements found in similar high mountain regions of Alaska and Canada. The report herein of a major avalanche seems to have been an aberration for the regular climbing season on the regular route. It is appropriate and of interest for this journal, of course. In the future, we expect more reports from Mexico, including places like the Barranca de Cobre and Baja. For the time being, we are not printing a data base in the Tables section.

There were a number of reports from the mid-Atlantic and New England regions that were difficult to draw conclusions from. For instance, we don't know what caused a rock climbing instructor to fall to his death from a cliff in Maryland, other than that he was about to teach rappelling to a group of Explorer Scouts. We don't know what caused a young Massachusetts climber to fall to his death from Rose Ledges, a popular climbing cliff near Northfield; and the same in a similar incident at Ragged Mountain in Connecticut. We don't know what kind of "failed" knots were involved in two serious falls—one resulting in a flail chest and the other a fatality—at Seneca Rocks and Tohican Valley Park. The information comes in either as a short newspaper clip or a Case Incident Report (common to public land custodians) that focuses on how the rescue or recovery was handled. Therefore, and as usual, we only know that the activity of climbing was engaged in, but not the profile of the victim or the cause of the fall or failure. This is why we continue to solicit help in report gathering, and why we want our accident reporting format more widely used.

We must again emphasize that many accidents in the mountains are not related to the sport of climbing, but are characterized as such. The high density climbing areas, such as Joshua Tree National Monument (estimated 300,000 climber days—but don't know how many climbers, though it is reported that as many as 4,000 a day are there on big weekends), Boulder Canyon (no estimates), and the Shawangunks (about 11,000 climbers—but don't know how many climber days), have accidents that happen to climbers and non-climbers on and around the cliffs. These have to be reported as climbing accidents, and the custodians have to count them this way, even though the individuals may not be climbers, because the occurrence was on a well-defined climbing route. This is quite different from the individuals who fall from an overlook in Delaware Water Gap or wander from a trail in Yosemite or Rocky Mountain National Park and fall. Yet the latter are being counted as "mountaineering" or "mountain-related" accidents, and hikers as well as people who just step out of the car and into the mountain environment continue to be characterized as climbers. This is a tide difficult to stem.

In addition to the Safety Committee, we are grateful to the following individuals for collecting data and helping with the report: Peter Armington, Dennis Burge, Micki Canfield, Joseph Evans, George Hurley, Renny Jackson, Roger Robinson, Jeff Scheetz, Thomas Sheuer, and, of course, George Sainsbury.

John E. (Jed) Williamson
Editor, USA
7 River Ridge
Hanover, NH 03755

Orvel Miskiw
Editor, Canada
8631 - 34th Ave NW
Calgary, Alberta

CANADA

FALL ON ROCK, INADEQUATE PROTECTION, HASTE
Alberta, Rocky Mountains, Mount Yamnuska

On the morning of April 25, 1992, Craig E. and Rob G. registered out for a climb of the eight-pitch route "Red Shirt," about 270 meters high and rated 5.7, on Mount Yamnuska. About 12 hours later they had completed most of the climb and Craig started up the final pitch to the top of the face. He clipped into four pitons as he traversed a ledge, then moved out of view as he went around a corner and upward. Moments later, Rob and another party who had just reached the belay station heard Craig scream and them saw him fall into view and on down the face, crashing into it on the way. Three of the four pitons on the traverse pulled out before Craig was stopped by his rope.

After hearing sounds from the victim below, Randy S. rappelled down to him and found him to have a fractured wrist, a detached ear, and a serious injury to the back of the head (later diagnosed as a basal skull fracture). He secured Craig on a ledge, put additional clothing on him, and bandaged his head with a T-shirt before completing the climb with his partner Cam Q. to go for help. They left an extra rope for Rob, who stayed at the belay. Meanwhile, another climber hiking below had heard the commotion, and called Kananaskis Emergency Services with a portable radio. Rescuers were called into action from Kananaskis Central and West Districts, Canmore Helicopters, Yamnuska Mountain School, Canmore Ambulance, Canadian Parks Service, and civilian volunteers in the area.

A helicopter flew directly to the top of the route and let off three rescuers at 2125, and then was able to deliver four more and a load of equipment before darkness. At 2310, anchors were in place at the top of Red Shirt, and a rescuer was lowered to the victim. A half hour later Craig was raised to the top, and around 0015 his partner Rob was also brought up from his belay platform. Craig's condition was judged to be too serious to wait for helicopter evacuation at daybreak. He was secured to a spine board, loaded on a sled, and moved carefully down the back side of the mountain over snow and rock toward the trail. Because of his head injury, he had to be kept awake by continual prodding. Meanwhile, several other rangers, paramedics, and volunteers started up on foot from the parking lot with medical equipment and Cascade stretcher, which is equipped with a wheel. They met the first team, carrying the victim at 0150, transferred him to the Cascade, and began treatment with heat packs, oxygen, and saline I.V. before resuming his evacuation down the slopes of Yamnuska. They reached the road at 0430 (April 26) and an ambulance then transported the victim to Foothills Hospital in Calgary. He was released a week later with his ear reattached and good prospects of full recovery. (Source: Burke Duncan, Kananaskis Central District Ranger)

Analysis

Although no one saw what caused Craig to fall, that pitch is not as difficult as a number of others which he had already climbed, so it is speculated that he was too eager to finish the climb and did not pay enough attention to protecting the last section or to his holds on the rock. Most of his 30 meter fall was related to distance he climbed beyond the fixed pins on the traverse. Many accidents are caused by the tendency to 'jump the last step.' The provincial Alpine Specialist also points out the potential of cooperation among various agencies and trained volunteers as shown by this successful rescue mission. (Source: Orvel Miskiw)

FALL ON ROCK, INADEQUATE PROTECTION
Alberta, Rocky Mountains, Mount Yamnuska

On July 12, 1992, two Calgarians, R. V. and E. W., were climbing Corkscrew, a 5.8 multi-pitch route near the east end of the southeast face of Mount Yamnuska, when R. V., who was leading the third pitch around 1300, clipped into one of two fixed side-by-side pins without testing it. He then ran into difficulties and fell some 20 meters, pulling that piton along the way. He sustained head and neck injuries and became unconscious for several minutes. E. W. shouted for help, and was heard by other climbers nearby, and also by hikers below the cliff, who reported to Bow Valley Provincial Park Rangers.

While the rangers were organizing helicopter support in Canmore, as well as other resources for a rescue, two climbers on the cliff nearby abandoned their climb in order to help. They climbed up to the victim, and then with help from E. W., lowered him to the bottom of the rock face at 1500. There he was picked up on a sling by helicopter, and was transferred to the Canmore Ambulance at the climbers' parking lot where he was taken by ambulance to Canmore Hospital. (Source: George Field, Alpine Specialist, Peter Lougheed Provincial Park)

Analysis

Climbers occasionally fall while leading, as part of the appeal of the climbing sports is the opportunity to develop personal skills by taking on ever greater challenges. This is why good protection is essential. In this case, R. V. feels he had become too complacent about protection existing on climbing routes, and could have ensured or placed better protection if he had taken along his hammer and pitons. As well, he should have clipped into both pins at his last placement. Even if the other one appeared less reliable, it may have been able to stop his fall. However, he is pleased that he was wearing a full body harness, because he may not have survived hanging inverted for as long as he was on the rope due to his head injuries. Also, he stresses the importance of helmets in climbing. As his helmet was destroyed in the fall, he would likely have been fatally injured without it.

This incident also suggests the value of training in rope systems for hauling and lowering. In some cases, a belayer may not have helped in getting an injured partner to a safe resting position while awaiting rescue, which may be of vital importance in some injuries. (Source: Orvel Miskiw, with advice from R. V. and E. W.)

FALL IN CREVASSE, UNROPED, CLIMBING ALONE, INATTENTION
Alberta, Rocky Mountains, Mount Athabasca

Nick M. registered at the Columbia Icefield on July 21, 1992, for a solo climb of Mount Athabasca (3490 meters) the following day. He intended to start at 0530, follow the Silverhorn route to the summit, and descend by either the standard route or the Athabasca-Andromeda col. He was well equipped, had taken an ice climbing course, and had some mountaineering experience in South America and in the Coastal Range of British Columbia. At 1900 on July 22, the Icefield Centre staff reported that Nick had not returned his registration, and a Park Warden began an investigation. He located the overdue climber's car in a parking lot and determined that he had been seen by other climbers on route near the summit at 1230 that day. Nick's room at the Icefields Chalet was checked for overnight gear, and a description was obtained from staff. Descent routes were scanned from various vantage points until dark without result.

The next day, an aerial search of the mountain located tracks below the headwall of the A-A Col. They led to a collapsed snow bridge over a crevasse. A rescue party was slung down to the site, and they were able to see a ski pole deep in the crevasse. A Park Warden was then lowered into the hole and discovered Mr. M. wedged upside down, about 20 meters from the surface. He had died, apparently from hypothermia.

Analysis
Climbing alone on glaciers is a high-risk activity. The narrow crevasse into which Nick had fallen was not hidden; open sections were visible on either side of the snow bridge on which he tried to cross, and he should have been able to jump or even step across it. It appeared that he was following older tracks in the snow, but recent warmer temperatures had probably weakened the bridge. Travel was made somewhat more strenuous by recent new snowfalls, and this may have contributed to a poor route selection decision by the victim. (Source: Terry Damm, Jasper National Park Warden Service)

LOSS OF CONTROL—VOLUNTARY GLISSADE, UNROPED
Alberta, Rocky Mountains, Mount Fisher
Fisher Peak (3053 meters) was the day's objective for Thomas W. (36) on July 22, 1992. He bicycled in from Elbow Falls with his friend J. M. to get close to the mountain as quickly as possible, and then they set off on foot up Shoulder Creek to approach the mountain from the east. Around 1430, the pair were traversing a cirque around the 2600 meter level when they encountered steep slabs which they had to descend. Thomas decided to slide down, but the slabs were covered with loose rocks and he lost control, then tumbled out of sight of his partner. He came to rest 100 meters below, on a scree slope. J. M. made his way down to the victim and found him unconscious, with erratic pulse, head and face injuries, scrapes and contusions on his body, and low, shallow breaths with gurgling sounds. Finding there was no more he could do for Thomas at the scene, J. M. hiked and bicycled back and reported the accident to Elbow Ranger Station at 1605. Immediately, the rangers began to assemble resources for a rescue. A helicopter was requested from the Alberta Forest Service nearby, and Bow Valley Provincial Park was notified that a sling-capable helicopter might be required. Also the Shock Trauma Air Rescue Society (STARS) in Calgary was informed, and their helicopter and crew were dispatched.

At the accident site about 1710, the AFS helicopter found it could not land at the bottom of the scree bowl below the victim's position due to gusting winds, so it dropped off two people at the valley bottom and tried again. But again it was unable to land, so it took everyone back to Little Elbow. Then the STARS helicopter attempted to land in the scree bowl, but it was also unable to do so. It returned to Little Elbow to wait for the sling helicopter and specialized mountain rescue team from Bow Valley. The Bow Valley unit arrived at Little Elbow about 1800, transferred appropriate gear, and lifted off for the accident site about 1825. It landed in a meadow below the scree bowl, and from there it transported two rangers, one at a time, to a location about 100 meters below Thomas. They reached him at 1900 and after checking him as thoroughly as possible, they agreed that he was dead. The body was loaded into a "Jenny" stretcher and lifted out on a sling by helicopter. As the winds had subsided by then, the machine was able to land in the scree bowl upon its return and pick up the rangers. (Source: D. Humphrey, Kananaskis County East District Ranger)

Analysis
Thomas was an experienced scrambler, but while like most scramblers, his aspirations expanded to great challenges like Mount Fisher, it seems he did not acknowledge the greater hazards those might present. Even talented enthusiasts would do well to associate any of the available alpine clubs or mountain schools for a while, even if only to learn the sort of fear which could have averted this tragic accident. (Source: Orvel Miskiw)

STRANDED, OFF ROUTE, EXCEEDING ABILITIES
Alberta, Rocky Mountains, Mount Temple
On August 6, 1992, Joe P. and Martin L. climbed the east ridge of Mount Temple (3544 meters) but stalled at 2000 when they reached the Black Towers, unsure if they were on route. They bivvied overnight and tried to continue in the morning. After climbing part way up a gully, they found they could not make any more headway because of bad weather and loose rock, and could not climb down from their position either. With darkness approaching, they tried to send an SOS signal by headlamp to the lodge at Moraine Lake. Their signal was seen and the Banff Park Warden Service was contacted. A search was initiated at first light on August 8, and the pair were located in the Black Towers around 3200 meters. They were rescued by helicopter. (Source: Banff National Park Warden Service)

Analysis
These climbers were experienced, but had route-finding problems and were uncomfortable with the type of rock they encountered. Acquiring further information on the climb before attempting it may have kept them from getting off route. The Black Towers have often been climbed straight on, so they are not necessarily 'off route,' except to someone who has heard about bypassing them and intends to do so; it's doubtful that they present climbing as difficult as the Big Step lower on the mountain, so anyone who gets over that should have no trouble negotiating the towers. However, by the time most climbers reach them, they feel the worthwhile part of the climb is behind and want only to get off it, walk to the summit, and then get off the mountain. The Black Towers therefore represents an ominous and unwelcome complication, best bypassed through gullies to the left. (Source: Orvel Miskiw)

FALLING SNOW BLOCK, FALL ON ROCK AND ICE, INADEQUATE BELAY, POOR POSITION
Alberta, Rocky Mountains, Mount Temple
On September 1, 1992, two Americans, Doug S. and Mike V., set out to climb the East Ridge of Mount Temple. Early fall snows had left the mountain in winter condition, but the climbers proceeded without incident until they reached the exit gullies that bypass the Black Towers. The choice of the wrong gully, and then verglas on the rock, made for challenging climbing. The climbers were on the last pitch before exiting through a cor-

nice onto the summit ridge when Doug, the leader, ran out of protection for a belay. They agreed to move together with the protection of their immediate placements, and Mike unclipped from the lower station. While digging through the cornice, Doug dislodged a large snow block, which went down the gully and struck Mike. He fell about five meters and injured his leg before Doug stopped him. Both climbers then struggled to the top of the gully and up the ice cap to the summit. Part way down the descent, Mike felt he could not continue, so Doug left him and went on alone for help. He contacted the Banff Park Warden Service in Lake Louise at 2400, and a rescue plan was made for the morning. At daylight, the victim was found, stabilized, and slung out by helicopter to an ambulance waiting at Moraine Lake. He was found to have a fractured fibula. (Source: Banff National Park Warden Service)

Analysis
The two were experienced mountaineers; however, they chose the wrong gully to reach the summit ridge. Bad weather, causing poor visibility, may have been a factor. The correct gully, right of the one they ascended, may have been easier.

It appears that Mike's leg was broken in the fall, rather than by the snow block. An initial free fall on slack rope places a greater load on the belayer. They are both lucky that Doug was able to hold it from his precarious position. (Source: Orvel Miskiw)

CORNICE COLLAPSE, UNROPED, BAD WEATHER, OFF ROUTE AT NIGHT
Alberta, Rocky Mountains, Mount Temple
On September 12, 1992, James H. (38) and Charles B. (30) met at Moraine Lake to climb the East Ridge of Mount Temple. They set off at 1300, intending to bivouac above the Big Step and finish the climb the following day. They bivvied as planned and resumed the climb at 0800 on September 13. Early snows had encased the mountain in winter conditions, making the climbing slow and difficult, so that the climbers did not reach the summit until 0400 September 14. Due to blizzard conditions, they started down from the summit right away, but unfortunately went the wrong way, taking a rib that led them toward the north face rather than the northeast ridge, the normal descent route. They started out roped up, but soon dispensed with the rope as the traveling appeared to be straightforward. Both continued to wear their crampons over the snow and rock. James slipped and fell into a cornice. It collapsed and he slipped over the edge.

Charles looked for James for a while, but could not spot him, so he resumed the descent to get help. As it was getting light, he then realized that he was on the wrong ridge, so he crossed over to the correct one and continued. By that time, the climbers were overdue, and National Parks Wardens had commenced a search. Charles was picked up by helicopter and evacuated to Moraine Lake at 0800. The search team later spotted James' body at the bottom of the north face of Mount Temple. The cornice which had collapsed under him was right at its apex. The body was slung out to Lake Louise later that morning.

Analysis
James was an experienced mountaineer with many winter ascents, and both climbers were well prepared. But both were fatigued after some 20 hours of continuous climbing, and James was not wearing his prescription glasses due to blowing snow and the cold,

whereas he had previously always worn them. Bad weather and the darkness may have also contributed to the wrong choice of route for the descent. (Source: Banff National Park Warden Service)

SLIP ON SNOW, UNROPED, HASTE
Alberta, Rocky Mountains, Three Sisters, Big Sister
About 1315 on September 30, 1992, Richard O. and Jim B. were hurrying upward in strong winds on the southwest slopes of the third Sister (2937 meters) when Richard slipped on a small patch of snow and fell about six meters. He sustained injuries suspected to be a broken left leg and right ankle. Jim tried to help Richard down the mountain, but his injuries were too severe. Jim made him as comfortable as possible and went down alone for help. He reached the Spray Lakes Ranger Station at 1430.

Rangers from Bow Valley and Peter Lougheed Provincial Parks were soon transported to the accident site by a unit from Canmore Helicopters, using the sling method. They treated Richard, immobilized his injuries, and then slung him down to an ambulance waiting at the road.

Analysis
Rangers determined from discussion with the climbers that they seemed overconfident and were moving fast, perhaps too fast. The strong wind blowing at the time also contributed to the accident. Use of a rope in exposed or tricky sections may have averted the accident, while costing them little more time. This is the first accident reported on a route described in a new guide book of mountain scrambles. Scramblers need to read the fine print in this book and appropriately evaluate their choice of route. (Source: George Field, Alpine Specialist, Peter Lougheed Provincial Park)

RAPPEL ANCHOR FAILURE, FALL ON ICE
Alberta, Rocky Mountains, Tangle Ridge, Centre Stage Falls
Around mid-day on November 26, 1992, Pat S., who was a Park Warden, Mountain Guide, and Public Safety instructor with the Canadian Parks Service in Jasper National Park, and Lisa P., a warden from Banff National Park, left their vehicle to hike in to an ice climb on the west slope of Tangle Ridge, about 100 kilometers south of Jasper. Their objective was a 50 meter sheet of ice known as "Centre Stage." They were out for an easy recreational climb on their day off and Lisa's first attempt at waterfall ice.

After bushwhacking to reach the ice, the ascent was made routinely, and Pat lowered Lisa along the north side of the climb from a three-point anchor. Then he moved across to the south side of the ice to set up an anchor for which he used a single 30 centimeter piece of conduit. Lisa saw the ropes come down from the top, although Pat was out of sight on an upper step of the formation, about 50 meters above her. Seconds after the rappel ropes dropped, she saw Pat fall to the base of the climb. She assessed his injuries and used a radio from his pack to alert the Jasper Park Warden Office to the situation. At 1550, wardens at the nearby Sunwapta Station monitored her call and began to respond. The initial report of the victim's injuries included a broken femur, a head injury, cracked ribs, and a fractured wrist, but while the closest rescue party was still *en route*, the report changed: first to difficulty breathing, then to loss of consciousness, then lack of pulse. Lisa began CPR immediately and maintained her efforts for over 45 minutes until the first party arrived on foot to assist. The Canadian Parks Service contract helicopter, racing against the approaching darkness from its base in Valemont, B.C., reached the area a few minutes later and within ten minutes the victim was evacuated to the advanced life support unit waiting below. A back-up helicopter and rescue team from Banff, only minutes behind the first machine, had to set down at the Columbia Icefields for the night. A pulse was never restored, and Pat was declared dead on arrival at the hospital in Jasper.

Analysis
Public Safety Specialists from both Banff and Jasper investigated the accident site around 1300 the next day. Only the one anchor point could be found at the victim's rappel station. He had been no more than four or five meters into the rappel when the conduit pulled out. A deformity at one end of the tube may have been caused by impacting on rock. The ice was warm and wet, and it is believed that similar conditions the previous day may have contributed to the failure. It appears that this mature veteran of many underwater, underground, and mountaineering exploits (and rescues) gambled on a one-point anchor. We think he would want you to know. (Source: Canadian Parks Service, Jasper National Park)

AVALANCHE, INADEQUATE EQUIPMENT, POOR POSITION, FAILURE TO HEED FORECAST
British Columbia, Rocky Mountains, Mount Field, Silk Tassel Falls
On February 2, 1992, two parties of two set out for Silk Tassel, a grade 4 ice climb near the Trans-Canada Highway. Around 1200, they hiked to its base and began the 55 meter ascent. The two were climbing side by side when an avalanche swept over the top. Its main flow hit one party directly, knocking the leader off the route and dragging his partner out of his belay station at the bottom. The edge of the slide poured over the leader of the second party, but he managed to hang on to his tools and did not fall.

He and his belayer descended the route and the avalanche debris and quickly found the other belayer, partly buried and quite dazed. They dug him out, and all proceeded down the gully until they found the boot of the leader sticking out of the debris. Then one member of the second party ran back to the road for help and a shovel, while the remaining two started digging the victim out with an ice ax.

As this was happening, an off-duty ambulance attendant observed the climbers digging in the fresh debris and radioed the Warden Service to report the accident. A party of wardens was dispatched and the attendant drove in to the Field to get his ambulance.

By the time the rescue team had arrived at the accident site, the victim had been dug out after being buried for an estimated 30 minutes, and the climbers were doing CPR on him. As slides were running continually, he was moved to a safer area, and CPR was continued until he could be evacuated by helicopter. He was transported to hospital, but was pronounced dead of suffocation. He had sustained chest injuries, which may have contributed to his death. His belayer was also evacuated by helicopter and found to have a cervical spine fracture and a concussion.

Analysis
Three of the four climbers were very experienced. The avalanche hazard was forecast low in the morning, rising to high or extreme as daytime warming progressed. The weather forecast called for a record-breaking high temperature, and that did occur. At the time of

the accident, it was 8 degrees C. The slope that avalanched was a low-elevation, southerly-aspect basin directly above the route, and wet avalanches were observed by the climbers before they started at noon. They did not have probes or shovels with them, and although they carried avalanche beacons, those were not activated. (Source: Terry Willis, Yoho National Park Warden Service)

CRAMPON SNAGGED, FALL ON SNOW, INADEQUATE EQUIPMENT (ICE AXES ON PACKS)
British Columbia, Rocky Mountains, Mount Dennis, Guinness Gully
A party of two climbed Guinness Gully, a multi-pitch grade 4 ice route, on March 3, 1992. They then rappelled part of the way down the climb before traversing through some timber to a steep descent gully to the west. The descent gully is a small avalanche path, and an avalanche had run in it earlier in the year, leaving a smooth, hard track and debris at the bottom.

As the climbers approached the bottom of this gully at 1600, one of them snagged a crampon and fell forward. He rapidly picked up speed, passing his partner and sliding some 150 meters down the 25 degree slope before piling up in rocks, trees, and hard snow at the bottom. He sustained broken ribs, compound fractures to both ankles, and multiple lacerations to his arms. His partner ran the short distance to the road and drove to the park administration office to report the accident. A warden rescue team hiked in with medical and evacuation equipment. The victim was checked over and immobilized, and because of the steepness and roughness of the terrain, slung out by helicopter to an ambulance.

Analysis
The victim was the less experienced climber, but still quite experienced. It was reported that he was wearing a different pair of crampons than he normally used. As he was above and behind his partner when he fell, it is unlikely that the partner would have been able to stop him if they had been roped together. They did not have their ice axes available for a self-arrest, and that is possibly the most important single precaution which could have forestalled this accident. (Source: Terry Willis, Yoho National Park Warden Service)

ROPE PARTED (WORN THROUGH ON ROCK EDGE WHILE JUMARRING), FALL ON ROCK
British Columbia, Coast Mountains, Stawamus Chief
On April 8, 1992, Grace W. left her climbing partner near the south summit of Stawamus Chief in order to examine a wall for new route prospects. She was jumarring up the wall at 1415 when her nine mm rope apparently chafed through on a rock ledge. She fell 300 meters and was killed. Police, ambulance, fire department, and Provincial Emergency Program personnel located her body on a ledge and removed it by helicopter.

Analysis
The repeated motions involved in jumarring seem likely to aggravate any tendency for a sharp edge to damage a rope. To minimize the risk, climbers should use the thickest rope that will pass through the jumars, watch for sharp edges and pad them whenever possible. (Source: Ian Kay, Vancouver)

SLIP ON ICE, NO HARD HAT, INADEQUATE PROTECTION
British Columbia, Northern Selkirk Mountains, Mount Colossal

On August 7, 1992, during the third week of the annual ACC General Mountaineering Camp at Fairy Meadows in the Adamants, the chief guide, Don V., a long-standing member of the ACMG, was leading a party of two rope teams on a climb of Mount Colossal (2940 meters). It usually involves a long traversing ascent of a steep snow slope, but this year low snowfall and warm weather left more rock and ice exposed than normal in this area, and that was the case on Mount Colossal. A talus slope at the bottom was followed by hard snow and steepening ice, possibly 50 degrees at the top.

While leading his group up this ice slope in threatening weather, from a belay about one rope-length above the rocks, Don cautioned them to take their time and watch the footing, but moments later he lost his own on a slope of more than 40 degrees after getting an ice block stuck between the front points of one crampon. He slid some 50 meters down the ice, unable to stop himself because of the hard surface, or be stopped by his party because he had placed no protection, until he ran into the rocks at the bottom. He suffered bruises, abrasions, lacerations to his legs and head, a twisted neck, and general soreness.

He was able to discuss the situation with his group and organize them to help him back to the camp. After being given first aid and suturing to his worst cuts, he stayed there overnight and was flown out by helicopter the next morning during the weekly Saturday exchange of clients, for medical examination. He was found to be not seriously injured, but took a couple of weeks off to recuperate. (Source: Various clients and leaders from the ACC GMC)

Analysis

The climb was being done in a common manner, so accidents like this could happen much more often than they do. A sloping sheet of ice is a bad place for a slip without protection because it is often impossible to self-arrest, even for a professional mountaineer, and especially for a roped party, where one person could take down the rest. When a slip happens, the little extra time taken to place even one ice screw per rope-length may suddenly prove to have been a good investment. Also, the victim was not wearing his helmet, and in view of the exposure and his eventual head injury, it would have been appropriate. (Source: Orvel Miskiw, with advice from C. Shokoples, ACMG Guide)

SLIP ON ICE, INADEQUATE BELAY, INATTENTION, FATIGUE
British Columbia, Coast Mountains, Tahumming Glacier

For Bob P. and Doug W., August 28, 1992, was day eight of a 21-day traverse of the Tahumming Horseshoe near the head of Toba Inlet. Their objective for the day was to cross a small hanging glacier, find a route down an icefall, and then cross Tahumming Glacier to reach its west flank. After two attempts to find a way down the icefall, they still faced impassable obstacles and so decided to go back up to camp on easier terrain overnight, before reconnoitering the area for alternatives the next day. They had 15 meters of rope between them, and each was carrying 18 meters of rope and a large pack. At 1600 they were ascending diagonally on steep ice with patches of snow, and numerous crevasses around them, when Bob lost his footing on the ice. He landed on his back and started to slide.

Although he quickly rolled over into self-arrest position, his fatigue and the smoothness of the ice made it impossible to stop. When he reached a crevasse, he struck its footwall, fracturing both legs and a wrist, then fell some two meters into the crevasse, where he was held in his harness by Doug's rope. Fortunately, Doug had seen him fall and had time to take a strong belay stance.

As Bob was conscious, the two were able to discuss their problem. In the next hour and a half, Doug set up anchors, splinted Bob's legs, and hauled him up to the surface. They were carrying an FM transceiver with several frequencies, and were able to get a distress message out to the B. C. Forest Service, communicating directly with their Powell River office. A Canadian Forces Labrador helicopter reached them at 1900, and the two climbers were evacuated to Comox by 2015. (Source: The injured climber, Bob P.)

Analysis
Bob is glad that he and Doug had practiced crevasse rescue thoroughly before their trip, had considered the problems of rescue and evacuation in the remote areas they would be in, and had carried a two-way radio in case of emergency. But he feels that the accident could have been prevented by paying a little more attention to his footing. One lesson to be skimmed off this accident is that in some cases, a little extra caution is better than any amount of emergency equipment. (Source: Orvel Miskiw)

RAPPEL SLING ANCHOR UNTIED, FALL ON ROCK
Quebec, Mount Cesaire
On July 2, 1992, a group of 15 from the Monteregie Youth Center in Chambly, including four group leaders, plus two instructors from the Quebec Mountaineering Federation (FQM), went out to a cliff on Mount Cesaire for climbing practice. First the instructors set up top ropes on five routes, and both of them checked all the anchors and knots before descending to supervise the climbing, belaying, and lowering. The youngsters climbed these routes all morning and into the early afternoon, and four of them had climbed the route "Unnamed" and been lowered safely to the bottom by 1300. Then Patrick L. took his turn, and after reaching the top, was being lowered on a pulley by a supervised belayer at the bottom when he fell some 18 meters to the ground, sustaining fractures of the right wrist, upper arm, collarbone, and shoulder.

After the leaders and instructors determined that Patrick was conscious, one instructor, Yves B., went for help. He called Dominique F., who contacted the Quebec Police and the Ambulance Service before going to meet him with a rescue stretcher. She then accompanied the police to the scene of the accident while Yves waited for the ambulance. Ten minutes later, it arrived and he and the paramedics followed. They administered first aid and immobilized the victim for transport to the ambulance.

Seeing everything was in hand, the instructors went to the top of the pitch to find out what had gone wrong. They found the knot in the anchor sling had come untied. The knot had apparently slipped loose, unlikely as that seemed, seeing as it had been well tied. That was the only possible explanation, since all the other equipment was intact.

While the other instructor, Thierry B., stayed at the cliff to supervise the rest of the group and review the accident as much as possible, the victim was evacuated, and a group leader and Yves accompanied him to the hospital, where Patrick was kept overnight for observation. (Source: Denis Gravel, Quebec Mountaineering Federation)

Analysis
This accident reinforces the importance of backing knots up and of checking anchor set-ups periodically, especially when they are out of sight. It is also a common practice to use two or three anchor points for rappels. (Source: Orvel Miskiw)

STRANDED, EXCEEDING ABILITIES, LOST, DAMAGED AND INADEQUATE EQUIPMENT
Yukon Territory, Mount Logan
At 1530 on May 21, 1992, the Kluane National Park Warden Service received word from a local pilot that a group of four Italian climbers on the Hummingbird Ridge of Mount Logan (6050 meters) had broadcast a "mayday" and were requesting helicopter assistance.

Pilot Doug Makkonen from Trans North Turbo Air used a Bell 206 Jet Ranger to reach the mountain by 1945. The rescuers met two climbers at their 1800 meter base camp who were in radio contact with two stranded on the ridge. The two on the ridge claimed to have lost most of their snow protection, broken one crampon, and severely dulled their ice climbing tools in getting to where they were now. The climbing was severe enough that they felt they could neither downclimb nor continue ascending safely, but they could be reached by helicopter.

The rescue team decided to fly up to their location and assess the situation. The altimeter in the helicopter read 4740 meters when the climbers were spotted on a small corniced platform on the steep ridge, 1200 meters below the summit. They had their packs on and told the helicopter party over the radio that they would like to be picked up and taken down. However, a Bell 206 can barely maintain a slow fly-by at that altitude, let alone a landing and subsequent take-off. The helicopter descended to the base camp to discuss the rescue options, and it was decided best to allow each climber to attach himself to the end of a long fixed line while the machine hovered above.

The helicopter was stripped of all unnecessary weight, including back seat, headsets, and tools. The pilot then took it up alone to the climbers while the wardens explained to them by radio that they must leave their equipment behind, be sure they were not tied in to the mountain, and clip in to the sling line one at a time. Each climber in turn was then slung down to their camp. Neither one was injured.

Analysis
The two climbers were fortunate in that they had radio communication with their base camp, and to the outside, to request help when they needed it, that the helicopter was available, that the weather was ideal at the time, and that they were at an elevation that was within the limits for any sort of helicopter rescue. Since they had ascended 3000 meters in just two days, it's quite possible that they were already experiencing symptoms of altitude sickness. If they had had to wait any length of time for assistance, they might have been forced to either downclimb with inadequate equipment or succumb to the effects of altitude.

To climb in the St. Elias Mountains, where the closest aircraft assistance is, at best, an hour's flight away through mountainous terrain, where week-long storms are rather common, and where one can quickly ascend to an altitude where helicopter rescue may not be possible in even the best of conditions, one must be prepared for, and fully capable of, self-rescue. (Source: Andrew Lawrence, Kluane National Park Warden Service)

FALL INTO CREVASSE
Yukon Territory, St. Elias Mountains

On June 13, 1992, a group of five climbers and two guides were ascending an unnamed 3600 meter mountain east of McArthur Peak. At 0500 at the 2700 meter level, a series of large crevasses were encountered. After checking the route, the guides considered that a fixed line and a belay from the uphill side would adequately protect the group while they crossed. As the first two climbers were being belayed, one of the crevasse bridges collapsed and they both fell into it. While one guide held them on belay, the other went to the edge of the crevasse to check on the two who fell. P. S. was suspended by a rope about eight meters above the bottom of the crevasse, while R. V. was in a semi-sitting position on the crevasse floor, moaning and complaining that his right leg was broken. The other three climbers, downhill of the crevasses, were essentially OK, although P. W. had been knocked around by falling blocks.

P. S. was belayed out of the crevasse and, with two other clients, descended back to their high camp to make the 0800 radio schedule and report the accident. Guide J. B. rappelled into the crevasse to attend to R. V., and discovered fractures of the tibia and fibula of his right leg. Demerol was administered to relieve the extreme pain. By 0700 the leg was splinted, and by 0800 R. V. had been raised out of the crevasse. The clients returned to the accident site by 0900 with evacuation equipment, and R. V. was back in camp by 1200.

About 1400, Kluane National Park Wardens arrived by helicopter to transport R. V. and P. W. (who had sustained a head injury during the event) back to the Haines Junction nursing station.

Analysis

This accident was mostly the result of a bit of bad luck in uncertain conditions. The guides recognized the dangers and made a reasonable attempt to prevent such a mishap. The group was also fully prepared for self-rescue, resulting in a fairly straightforward evacuation of its injured members. (Source: Andrew Lawrence, Kluane National Park Warden Service)

MEXICO

AVALANCHE, FALL ON SNOW AND ICE
Puebla, El Pico de Orizaba

On November 16, 1992, a group of eight climbers began the standard route, Glacier de Jamapa, on the north slope of the mountain. The party of eight included two guides, Octavio Juarez and Tim Villanueva, and their clients, Kurt Dreibholtz, David Kristensen, Dick Nelson, Bob Roberts, Mike Randall and James Stevenson. The second party members were Rolando Montemyor and Bernardo Zuiga. The climbers left the Piedra Grande Hut at 0200. They reached the glacier about 0430, put on crampons, and shortly after the party of eight roped up into two teams of four. The other party of two continued unroped. The roped team led by Octavio Juarez climbed ahead, followed by the team of two as they were climbing a little faster than the second rope team led by Tim Villanueva. At one point the six climbers ahead climbed out of sight from the second rope team as the route rounds the ridge slightly toward the crater rim.

About 0845 around 4,500 meters (17,712 feet) as the lead group was diagonally ascending, a crack appeared in the two to four inch firm crust. The team members immediately secured their ice axes and watched the surface crust below them release. Moments passed, and, as they thought they were safe, a secondary release from above occurred. The slab hit each team member and the second team of two unroped climbers knocking them off their feet and into a tumbling fall along with the moving snow and ice. They fell about 700 meters to the base of the Chichimeco Glacier.

The second roped party did not see the fall. Their team was hit by a piece of snow and ice. At the time it did not seem likely that the ice came from the team above because the angle of the first party's route and the estimated distance between parties did not correspond. The second party chose to descend to the base of the Jamapa Glacier and wait for the first party to descend. About one hour and 45 minutes later, Tim Villanueva heard voices below and to the east. It was Kurt Dreibholtz and Bob Roberts who survived the fall. Dreibholtz was hurt but could walk; Roberts couldn't walk and was suffering from shock. They both said Octavio Juarez, David Kristensen, Rolando Montemyor and Bernardo Zuniga were lifeless. Tim Villaneuva responded to the injuries of Dreibholtz and Roberts. He planned and executed an emergency evacuation plan with the help of two other American climbers, Jeff Selleck and Douglas Neighbor and two German climbers, Alfred Menzel and Frommknect Lutz, who were at the hut. The entire group helped evacuate Dreibholtz and Roberts to the hut where they were transported by vehicle to Tlachichucha and on to the hospital in Jalapa.

Analysis

It is suspected that around 5,400 meters with the change in aspect from north to slightly northeast and with a slightly lower slope angle of the area near the crater rim, the melt/freeze cycle produced a surface crust that may have been in transition. The fall occurred at an area referred to as "The Crevasses." Though they were well filled in, it may be that the terrain change under the surface snow could have added to the weakness.

November is considered the ideal month for climbing because the bare ice is most likely to be covered by desirable snow. The 1992 wet season lasted longer than normal, with squalls of short storms continuing into October. There was no measurable new snow for at least several days prior to the accident, and no unusually high winds or obvious recent transport of snow. Several parties had climbed the route each day prior to the accident. Their tracks were visible and distinct. The party of eight had ascended the two other highest peaks of Mexico (Iztaccihuatl and Popocatepetl) the days before on similar aspects of slopes. They observed no avalanche activity and experienced desirable snow conditions. On the lower part of the route they experienced no unusual snow conditions with the steps being about boot-top deep. There was no evidence of avalanche activity. The snow conditions produced a favorable response to probing tests and quick ice axe shear tests.

Of the rope team, the first and third were killed. Both the two unroped climbers were killed. All who died were killed by fatal blows and were on the surface of the debris. They did not die from suffocation. At the hospital in Jalapa, Dreibholtz was diagnosed with multiple lacerations, snow blindness, frostbite, muscle and soft tissue trauma on left groin, hip, knee and leg and Roberts was diagnosed with multiple skin lacerations, severe muscle trauma on the left shoulder, rupture of left ligament and probable lesions of inner meniscus of the right knee. Villanueva's response to the accident was responsible for saving the lives of Dreibholtz and Roberts.

A group of about 40 climbers from Socorro Alpino of Mexico, the Red Cross of Jalapa, and climbing friends of Octavio Juarez efficiently managed the recovery of the bodies who remained on the mountain. Several local expert climbers who were involved with the body retrieval considered this a very unusual incident. The rescue leader considered it possibly a one-in-one hundred year occurrence. (Source: Bela G. Vadasz, Mountain Guide)

UNITED STATES

HAPE, FROSTBITE, INADEQUATE EQUIPMENT, WEATHER
Alaska, Mount McKinley

On April 24, 1992, Daryl Hinman (44), Tom Roseman (42) and Bob Rockwell (56)—members of the China Lake (CA) Mountain Rescue Group—started out from Kantishna to do a traverse of Mount McKinley, going up McGonagall Pass to the Muldrow Glacier, over Denali Pass, and down the West Buttress. We could climb the summit from Denali Pass. We expected to take three weeks.

The weather was colder than usual, and we crossed a frozen Wonder Lake and the McKinley River with ease. We reached McGonagall Pass (5,720 feet) on the 28th and dropped to the Muldrow. By May 3 we were at 11,000 feet starting up Karstens Ridge, the crux of the climb. Karstens Ridge is a knife edge in places, and ascends quite steeply in others: a lot of exposure. But the snow conditions were good for climbing. Also, we were able to clip into old fixed ropes for some protection in several spots.

On May 7 we started up gentler terrain on the Harper Glacier from our camp at 14,600 feet. Tom Roseman began to experience a serious lack of energy, but had no other symptoms. We attributed it to a touch of acute mountain sickness, and the fact that we had had no rest days in our two weeks on the mountain.

By the end of the next day we had managed only 3,000 feet higher and three miles. Tom was considerably weaker, and now exhibited a high resting pulse. Still, we did not suspect HAPE because he felt fine otherwise: good appetite, no lung sounds or coughing, and his breathing rate was normal.

On May 9, even though it was cloudy with winds of 30 knots and higher gusts, we had to move over Denali Pass. In an unfortunate accident on May 5 we had lost a gallon of fuel, and now had only enough for three or four more days. We needed to be on the west side of the mountain in a descent mode in case this was the beginning of one of the infamous Denali storms.

We started out at noon in subzero temperatures. Tom's lack of energy was worse than before. Resting for 20 hours had not helped him at all. We stopped often and yet the stops did not help. (He stated later that keeping going was the hardest thing he has ever done.)

We reached Denali Pass around 1400 and headed down the steep west side for a place to camp. Even in descending Tom was lethargic. Soon it got icy and only the points of our crampons pierced the snow. After a couple of falls, the longest of which was 180 feet, we anchored and belayed each step of the way. But the anchors were not always secure, and a fall could be a serious event. Miraculously, we were not injured.

Finally, at 2200, we found a filled-in section on a crevasse at 17,400 feet, big enough for the tent. It had taken us eight hours to descend 800 feet! The temperature was -25° F with a wind chill of -87° F. We were cold and exhausted. Tom had a coughing spell and although it was a dry cough, we thought for the first time of the possibility of HAPE. Also, half of his left foot was frostbitten, as were my toes and fingers.

The next day we discussed going for help or continuing up on our own. But even if Tom had been able to move at a normal rate, it would have taken two more days to reach the Kahiltna landing strip. And two more days in subzero weather would have a dire effect on Tom's and Bob's frostbite.

No mountain rescue person ever wants to be the subject of a rescue, and we were especially sensitive to the fact that many climbers on Denali who request help are in fact quite capable of getting out of their predicament themselves. Certainly we felt that as mountain rescue personnel we would be even more expected to do so. Nevertheless, this was a time where discretion was called for, so Hinman went for help at 1030 and hoped he would encounter climbers with a radio. Failing that, he counted on getting to the rangers' 14,200 foot camp in the afternoon.

Daryl passed other climbers but none had a radio. He reached the ranger camp around 1400 and reported the situation. Barely an hour later a Lama helicopter arrived at Tom's and Bob's location and hovered with the front points of each skid on our platform. The main rotor was missing the slope above by only a few feet. Two rangers got out and we climbed aboard. Within minutes we were reunited with Daryl at the 14,200 foot camp! We complimented the rangers on the ultra-fast response. As it turned out, the four-day storm brought four feet of snow at the Kahiltna strip and 100 mph winds on the summit. One ranger described it as the worst in ten years for that season and more typical of December, not May. Six climbers perished as a direct or indirect result of this storm; unfortunately, this was only the beginning of by far the worst year in history for fatalities on Denali.

Then came a second helicopter ride to the Kahiltna, a fixed wing trip to Talkeetna, and another to Anchorage. By 1900, Tom and Bob were at the Humana Hospital emergency room. There, Dr. Peter Hackett examined Tom, and after only a few seconds with the stethoscope, announced, "You've got High Altitude Pulmonary Edema!" Everything now seemed to fall into place, and we breathed a sigh of relief that Tom's HAPE had evidently not progressed to life-threatening levels as we climbed from 15,000 feet to Denali Pass at 18,200 feet.

I stayed in the hospital for two days and will recover completely. Tom left the hospital after a week and a half, and will probably lose the tip of one big toe. Hinman suffered some frost nip but did not require treatment and was able to hike down after four days, once the storm had subsided. (Source: Robert Rockwell)

Analysis

We practiced and trained seriously for this climb. Because we would be on the Muldrow side early in the season, we knew we had to be even more capable and independent. And, we were experienced: Rockwell had been to 24,600 feet, and had climbed Denali before. Hinman had climbed Mount Logan's east ridge (with Rockwell). While this was Roseman's first expedition, he had been on numerous ascents in California's Sierra Nevada; and he was physically the strongest of the three at the start of the climb.

We feel that our preparation—while it did not prevent the problems from happening—kept them from having far more serious outcomes. (Source: Robert Rockwell)

The Muldrow Glacier is rated an Alaskan grade #2 in Jon Waterman's book and because of this very subjective rating, this particular route is sometimes underestimated. Because of the isolation and length of the route, it can be a very difficult and unforgiving climb. The Mountaineering Rangers advised this group to take an extra stove and a CB radio. Having only one stove and limited fuel forced them into a problem of dehydration early into their climb that may have contributed to both their frostbite and high altitude sickness. Also, with a CB radio they possibility could have made contact when they first started having serious problems. This party was extremely fortunate that a high altitude helicopter was available to respond quickly. Without immediate rescue, their deteriorating condition would have forced a serious situation with a ground rescue. (Source: Daryl Miller, Mountaineering Ranger, Denali National Park)

FALL ON SNOW, INADEQUATE PROTECTION
Alaska, Mount McKinley
On May 10, 1992, at 1710, the "West Buttheads" expedition, Timothy Hagan (39) and Paul Kogelmann (33) were descending the headwall from the 16,200 foot camp. They were traveling roped and opted not to clip into the fixed lines. Kogelmann, leading, slipped and fell about 150 feet above the bergschrund. Timothy Hagan was unable to hold the fall, and the team fell 500-600 feet down the headwall. An American team performed first aid and placed Hagan's left arm into a sling. They then continued the descent at a slow rate.

At 1750, rangers reached Hagan and reported that he had suffered a broken left humerus and facial lacerations. At 1755 Hagan was flown in the Lama to the 14,200 foot camp, and then down to Kahiltna airstrip, where he was flown to Talkeetna, then to the Humana emergency room in Anchorage.

Analysis
There have been a number of falls contributed to not clipping into the fixed line on the "headwall" above the 14,200 foot camp. Most of the serious injuries could have been prevented by clipping in. The "West Buttheads" were no exception in this case. Climbers underestimate the angle of the headwall and the quickness required to self-arrest to prevent the team from sliding out of control. By clipping into the fixed line, this team could have avoided this serious climbing fall and a very expensive ride to the Humana ER in Anchorage. (Source: Daryl Miller, Mountaineering Ranger, Denali National Park)

(Editor's Note: In a letter from Timothy Hagan, we learned that another team member, Kim Hood (37), developed pulmonary edema at 11,000 feet and had to return to Kahiltna Base Camp and was flown out on May 2. Hagan further indicated that the fall from the headwall on May 10 was initiated by Kogelmann, who pulled Hagan off in the process, as he could not effect an ice axe arrest.

Hagan also provided this analysis: "I have learned never to over-estimate the climbing ability of my partner. Also, there are definite cases where it is much safer to climb without a rope! I have no doubt that I could have descended the headwall safely by myself. For some unknown reason, we chose not to clip into the fixed line, probably thinking that it would be more bother than it was worth. (We had used mechanical ascenders during the ascent.) I had planned to clip into one of the fixed anchors if Paul felt that he needed a belay. Nice theory." We appreciate Hagan's candid account.)

STRANDED, FATIGUE, PARTY SEPARATED, INADEQUATE EQUIPMENT, WEATHER
Alaska, Mount McKinley
"Expedition McKinley" a group from France, spent the night of May 10, 1992, at 17,000 feet on the West Buttress of Mount McKinley, without a stove. A stove had been cached

at 16,200 feet on the West Buttress. During the afternoon of May 11, Mr. Sement and Mr. Berthois attempted to descend to 16,200 feet to retrieve the stove, but turned back due to winds and poor visibility. They decided to descend to 14,000 feet via the "Rescue Gully" and return to 17,000 feet that evening with a stove. Because Ms. Sement (26) felt she was too tired to descend, a decision was made to leave her at 17,000 feet. There were no other parties there.

Mr. Sement and Berthois arrived at 14,000 feet at 1430. Berthois notified NPS Mountaineering Ranger Ron Johnson that Ms. Sement was alone at 17,000 feet without a stove, and that Mr. Sement and he were too tired to climb back to 17,000 feet.

A weather forecast received the morning of May 11 predicted that a severe storm would hit Mount McKinley later on. The storm had the potential to be the worst May storm in the past ten years. Winds of over 100 mph were predicted for elevations over 14,000 feet. Weather conditions at 14,000 feet at 1300 consisted of snow and blowing snow, winds gusting to 30 mph and up to 200 feet of visibility.

Given the weather forecast and the fact that Ms. Sement was without a stove, Johnson decided a rescue attempt was justified. The rescue team ascended the "Rescue Gully" and arrived at 17,000 feet at 1843. Ms. Sement was found in her tent, waiting for her companions. She was in good condition.

Conditions in the "Rescue Gully" were poor. Visibility was limited to 200 feet and route-finding was difficult. The rescue team decided that descending the West Buttress would be more exposed to the wind, but would provide more straightforward route-finding. Ms. Sement was placed on a rope between Culberson and Johnson. The team left 17,000 feet at 1915. The descent was hampered by wind gusts of 40 mph and very limited visibility. Sement slipped twice and her falls were arrested by Johnson and Culberson. The rescue team arrived at 14,000 feet at 2100. Ms. Sement was reunited with the rest of her expedition. The storm intensified and no rescue attempts could have been instigated until the evening of May 13, 1992.

Analysis

The members of Expedition McKinley showed poor judgment by caching a stove at 16,000 feet and then moving to 17,000 feet and establishing a camp without a stove. This decision could have resulted in a much more serious situation. Maintaining proper hydration is imperative at high altitude. It is also questionable as to whether other alternatives to splitting the group up leaving one ill-equipped member were adequately explored.

Mr. Sement was issued a citation for 36CFR 2.34A(4): "Disorderly Conduct—Creating a Hazardous Condition." (Source: Ron Johnson, Mountaineering Ranger, Denali National Park)

FALL INTO CREVASSE, UNROPED
Alaska, Mount McKinley

On May 11, 1992, Dave Fulton (31) and Robert Burns were descending from a carry to Windy Corner on the West Buttress back to their camp at 11,000 feet on the West Buttress of Mount McKinley. They were both traveling unroped, having deposited their rope at Windy Corner. About 1500, at 12,100 feet, Fulton fell into a crevasse that was somewhat hidden next to and parallel to the packed trail. As Fulton tumbled down into the four to five foot wide crevasse, he hooked a crampon 25 feet down which threw his shoulder against the crevasse wall creating a stemming position. He could not see any bottom to the crevasse and speculates that if he hadn't stopped, he would probably have been killed. Fulton was able to stem out on his own but sustained some injury to his right knee and right shoulder. Fulton was able to descend back to the landing strip on the Kahiltna Glacier without assistance.

Analysis
Burns had climbed on Mount McKinley several times in the past, but this was the first for Fulton. Traveling unroped on glaciated terrain is never a good idea, even with previous experience on the route. (Source: Roger Robinson, Mountaineering Ranger, Denali National Park)

EXPOSURE, FROSTBITE, FATIGUE, WEATHER, LOSS OF TENT CONTAINING FOOD, FUEL, CLOTHING, EQUIPMENT
Alaska, Mount McKinley
On April 22, 1992, the three member Korean "Pohang" party flew in to climb the Cassin Ridge on Mount McKinley. On May 4 they started the route at the base of the Japanese Couloir with 15 days of food. By May 9 they had reached their high camp at 17,700 feet. Their plans were to make a summit attempt the next day but strong winds were encountered forcing the three to begin construction of a snow cave. While working on the cave, they had their tent blow away which contained most of their food, fuel, and some clothing and climbing equipment.

The three were determined to ration what food and fuel they had left in order to wait out the weather. For over a week they were sustained on half a cup of rice powder and one quart of water per person per day. At some point while enlarging the snow cave they found some cached fuel which bolstered their supply. The weather finally improved enough on May 16 that the trio decided to make a summit push. The three only managed to ascend 30 meters before realizing they were too weak to continue in the cold, windy conditions. Upon returning to the cave, the leader Hyun Doo Kang (26) found he had frostbite on at least four fingers. They realized that they were too week to go up or down and thought seriously of requesting a rescue.

On May 16, the NPS Lama helicopter was involved in search efforts for two Italian climbers lost on the Cassin. At 1700, while Doug Geeting was making a fly over of the Cassin, he heard the distress call, "Helicopter, helicopter, helicopter." Geeting informed NPS Talkeetna of the distress calls, who in turn informed the Kahiltna basecamp operator Annie Duquette. At 1835, Duquette confirmed that the calls were coming from the '92 Korea Pohang party, who were at the 17,700 foot level on the Cassin. They reported that they had been without food for five days, their leader had AMS, four frostbitten fingers and was too weak to go up or down.

Weather on the 17th remained poor and continued poor until noon on the 18th, when Ranger Roger Robinson, flying with Doug Geeting, began orbiting the South Face where the Koreans were located. The NPS Lama arrived at the Korean location at 1400 where it encountered down drafts preventing a possible air drop of food and fuel. At 1610, the NPS Lama with Ranger Jim Phillips and pilot Bill Ramsey departed the Kahiltna airstrip for the Cassin. This time they encountered very little wind, and at 1620 an airdrop was attempted, but the cargo tumbled down the South Face. At 1630, Ramsey determined there was adequate room for landing, setting down at the 17,700 foot location about 50 feet down the slope from their snow cave. All three began to descend toward the helicopter from the uphill position, placing them in jeopardy of walking into the rotor blades. The helicopter had to lift off where Phillips was able to indicate a proper approach for one person at a time, picking up Kang first. The other members, Jae Chul Kim and Bong Gyoo Jun were picked up on subsequent landings, all being transported to the 14,200 foot Ranger Station on the West Buttress. At 1729 all three Koreans were picked up by the Army's Chinook helicopter at the 14,200 foot camp and transported straight to Humana Hospital in Anchorage.

Kang had frostbite to all ten fingers and three toes. The other members, Jun and Kim, received minor frostbite on several of their toes.

Analysis
In the weather conditions encountered, it is important to remember to collapse one's tent before leaving it to dig a snow cave. The subsequent loss of food and fuel in this case created a very serious dilemma. The three had indicated they would have tried to go either up or down if they could have received the air drop. Considering Kang's condition, this would have been very difficult.

During the rescue, their approach from the uphill side of the helicopter could have been fatal. Before approaching a helicopter, make sure the pilot has given the okay to proceed toward the ship. Never approach or exit a helicopter from the uphill side. (Source: Roger Robinson, Mountaineering Ranger, Denali National Park)

SNOWBRIDGE COLLAPSE, INADEQUATE EQUIPMENT, PROBE POLE
Alaska, Mount McKinley
On May 17, about 1600, a snowbridge over a crevasse collapsed while three members of the Je Ju University expedition were preparing a campsite around 15,000 feet on the West Buttress of Mount McKinley. Mr. Duk Sang Jang was uninjured and able to descend to 14,000 feet. At 1730, Jang notified Mountaineering Ranger Ron Johnson of the incident. Due to a language barrier it was difficult to ascertain the specific details of the incident. Because of another incident in progress on the Cassin Ridge, a decision was made to send NPS, VIPs Matt and Julie Culberson and volunteers Jim Wickwire and John Roskelley to the incident site. Johnson remained at the NPS Ranger Camp in order to stand by for the Cassin incident and provide backup for the crevasse rescue team.

The Culbersons left 14,000 feet at 1750 followed by Roskelley and Wickwire at 1800. Route finding was difficult due to poor visibility caused by snow and blowing snow. Wind gusts of up to 40 mph and a temperature of 0° F made the ascent to the crevasse site difficult. Around the same time, unknown to NPS personnel, four other members of the Je Ju University expedition left 14,000 feet to attempt a rescue of their companions. The rescue parties arrived at the site of the incident approximately 1920.

They found that the collapsed snowbridge had exposed part of a crevasse that was approximately 40 feet wide, 200 feet long and 60 feet deep. A staging area for the rescue was established on the downslope side of the crevasse on a slope angle of about 35 degrees. Because of concerns about the language barrier and the skill and condition of the Korean rescue team, it was requested that they not become actively involved in the rescue.

Mr. Seong Yu Kang (26) was observed in the bottom of the crevasse. He was upright but buried to his chest by the debris from the collapsed snowbridge. The rescue team was concerned about the unstable snow conditions, the overhanging upper wall of the crevasse and the possibility that the debris that made up the floor of the crevasse was unstable. They decided that it was reasonable to descend into the crevasse. Matt Culberson and Roskelley were belayed into the crevasse. They were able to dig Mr. Kang out of the debris. He was then extricated from the crevasse by Julie Culberson, Wickwire and one of the Korean climbers. A "Z" pulley rescue system was used to facilitate the extrication. Mr. Kang was uninjured.

Culberson and Roskelley then located Mr. Dong Choon Seo (27), who was on his side and partially buried by the debris. His foot and shoulder were exposed. His head was partially buried by a block of snow.

Culberson and Roskelley realized that they would need additional help and a litter to facilitate Mr. Seo's extrication. Johnson was notified of the request. He and volunteers Brian Okonek and Bruce Blatchley left 14,000 feet at 2030. The arrived at the incident site at 2130 with additional rescue gear, including a SKED litter. Culberson and Roskelley, using a shovel and snowsaw, worked to free Mr. Seo from the snow debris. Mr. Seo was conscious and hypothermic with suspected internal injuries, including injuries to his lumbar spine and pelvis. He also had lacerations on his head and in his mouth. Because the weather was still poor with continued snowfall, Culberson used his body to shield and protect Mr. Seo.

About 2150, Blatchley descended to 14,000 feet with Mr. Kang and three members of the Korean rescue team. They were suffering from mild hypothermia and their presence made working at the incident site difficult.

Johnson prepared the SKED and lowered it into the crevasse. Culberson and Roskelley packaged Mr. Seo into a sleeping bag and then placed him into the SKED. About 2220, Mr. Seo was extricated from the crevasse by Julie Culberson, Wickwire, Okonek and Johnson using a "Z" pulley system. Matt Culberson and Roskelley were able to climb out of the crevasse.

While some members of the rescue team attended to Mr. Seo, the other members dismantled the raising system and set up a snow lowering system. The team then lowered Mr. Seo to 14,000 feet. The lowering required two 300 foot technical lowers and was hampered by bad weather and poor visibility. The team arrived at the NPS Ranger Camp at 2330, where Mike Young, M.D., and Dan Mazur were waiting. Mr. Seo's suspected problems included: hypothermia, cold injury to his feet, internal injuries, and injury to the pelvis. Mr. Seo was rewarmed, I.V. fluids were administered, a Foley catheter was inserted, and oxygen was administered. The evaluation and medical procedures were done under difficult conditions. Light was provided by three small flashlights, some of the medical equipment had to be improvised and modified, and the language barrier with the patient made assessment difficult. Mr. Seo was monitored throughout the night by Young and Mazur. From 0300 until 0900, Johnson and the Culbersons took shifts working with Young and Mazur.

On May 18, 1992, a break in the weather allowed Mr. Seo to be flown from 14,000 feet to 7,000 feet aboard the NPS Lama helicopter. At 7,000 feet, Mr. Seo was transferred to 210 Air National Guard Pavehawk helicopter. He was flown to Humana Hospital in Anchorage, where he was diagnosed as having severe dehydration, a bruised liver, severe tongue lacerations, minor frostbite to his feet and other minor injuries.

Analysis
Carefully probing for crevasses while on belay is important to do before establishing a camp. Given the thickness of the snow bridge which collapsed, it is possible that probing

with only an ice axe would not have revealed a crevasse. This builds a strong case for using longer probe poles when traveling on Alaska glaciers, particularly in heavily crevassed areas.

Additional Note: Seo attempted suicide while in the crevasse by biting his tongue. It was later learned through an interpreter that Seo was in a great deal of pain, and without being able to move attempted to commit suicide by the only means possible. His tongue had numerous deep lacerations, some full thickness, which were described by attending physicians as his most serious wounds. The tongue injuries had compromised his airway. (Source: Ron Johnson, Mountaineering Ranger, Denali National Park)

(Editor's Note: This narrative is included primarily to indicate the level of complexity involved in some rescue efforts. Furthermore, without the good will and skills of the other climbers—quite noteworthy ones in this case—and VIPs, the victim might not have survived.)

FALL ON SNOW, DESCENDING UNROPED, EXCEEDING ABILITIES
Alaska, Mount McKinley
At approximately mid day on May 20, 1992, Soo Yang Yung (29), Sung Tak Hong (26) and Seong Jong Jin (25) from Korea were killed while attempting to descend the Orient Express route on Mount McKinley. The three fell several thousand feet to the 15,800 foot level. On May 23, the three victims were extricated from the 15,800 foot location by the NPS contract LAMA helicopter and transported to the Kahiltna basecamp. From here they were flown to Talkeetna.

Analysis
A Fantasy Ridge guided party led by Chip Faurot was camped near the three at several of these locations. Faurot commented that he noticed the Koreans "were not comfortable on the terrain, especially exposed off camber ice." Faurot observed Hong fall several times while ascending Fantasy Ridge's fixed line at 12,800 feet. After several days of stormy weather, the three moved to 15,200 feet. The Koreans had plans to traverse down to the 14,200 foot camp on the West Buttress from their camp at 14,800 feet, but unfortunately found they were in the wrong place. On this same day, the three other members that were ascending the West Buttress made an attempt to meet up with the three on the Rib in order to give a hand assisting the Rib team down to the West Buttress route. It appears the three Rib climbers were not certain where they were on the route as discrepancies were discovered. Their reported locations were often 1000 feet off of what they told their West Buttress party compared to what was observed by Faurot. The three on the Rib indicated they were at 17,200 feet when actually they were at 15,200 feet. From May 14 through May 16, they encountered strong winds which kept them tent bound. By May 16, they reported two to three days of food left. The weather improved on the 27th where the three ascended to 16,200 feet. They took a rest day on the 18th where their West Buttress team suffered a serious crevasse collapse forcing the evacuation of one of their members. At an 0800 radio call on May 19, the Rib team indicated they would be making an attempt for the summit this day. Due to the circumstances with the accident the night before, the West Buttress team requested that the Rib team descend back to the 14,200 foot camp on the West Buttress. The Rib team declined and indicated they would try for the summit and hoped to be on top by 1600.

A group of NOLS instructors left for the summit on the same day as the Koreans. Willie Peabody of the NOLS group passed the Koreans at 16,500 feet on the 19th. The Koreans, like the NOLS group, had full packs and were planning on carrying everything to the plateau (19,500 feet), then descending the West Buttress. The NOLS group reached the plateau and encountered extremely cold and windy conditions with poor visibility. They descended the West Buttress after seeing the Koreans for the last time at 17,900 feet on the West Rib.

The West Buttress Koreans received no communication from the Rib team until 1000 on the 20th. On this call they reported that they had not reached the summit and were in a snow cave because of very strong winds. Their tent was damaged, they were out of food and indicated that they would be descending down to the 14,200 foot camp this day. This was the last communication with the Rib team. Since they were last seen at 17,900 feet, their camp was most likely high on the West Rib in a very exposed area.

This descent route is no easy escape route even in good weather without heavy packs. The trio succumbed as a result of making the same fatal mistake that has taken a dozen other climbers in the last 20 years. (Source: Roger Robinson, Mountaineering Ranger, Denali National Park)

SNOW LIP/BRIDGE COLLAPSE—FALL INTO CREVASSE, INADEQUATE BELAY, WEATHER
Alaska, Mount McKinley

On May 4, 1992, Mugs Stump (41)—a guide for Mountain Trip—and his clients Nelson Max (40) and Robert Hoffman (45) began climbing the 1965 Japanese Ramp Route on the South Buttress of Mount McKinley. The team established a base camp on the upper part of the East Fork of the Kahiltna Glacier and made at least one carry of food and equipment up the Ramp before moving their camp onto the South Buttress. The Ramp, a steep and crevassed glacier that descends the South Buttress from 15,600 feet and feeds into the East Fork about 11,600 feet, is known for its objective hazards from crevasses, ice fall, and avalanches. On May 20, Stump and Max reached the summit of Mount McKinley via the Southeast Spur Finish in extremely adverse weather conditions.

On May 21, about 1130, Stump and his clients began their descent from high camp at 16,000 feet on the Southeast Spur in generally good weather. At 1300 they began descending the Ramp. First on the rope team was Hoffman, followed by Max, who was tied in a short distance behind, and Stump at the end of the rope with a greater length of rope between him and Max than between Max and Hoffman. There were no tracks left from their ascent, and Hoffman followed Stump's directions for route finding. They crossed a large slope beneath and slightly south of some seracs and an ice cliff as they approached a large crevasse. Hoffman stated he felt they were at a point further left of where they crossed this crevasse on their ascent. He stated that Stump had a sense of urgency to get off the slope and away from the avalanche path overhead. The air temperature had warmed and snow conditions were soft. Hoffman stopped near the edge of this crevasse, unsure of how to proceed. Stump approached the crevasse from uphill, passing by Max and Hoffman, to inspect the route. He was standing on the uphill lip of the crevasse and appeared to be inspecting a flimsy looking snowbridge. Hoffman said that he heard a "crack," and then Stump suddenly disappeared into the crevasse. He pulled in approximately 15 feet of slack rope between him and Max before Max was pulled off his feet. Max attempted to self-arrest, but was pulled toward the crevasse for approximately 20 feet before stopping. The rope between him and Stump became slack, and there was no longer force pulling Max down.

Max and Hoffman anchored the climbing rope. They attempted to contact Stump by yelling, but were without success. At this time, about 1330, the weather deteriorated with clouds and poor visibility. Feeling in a very precarious position on the uphill side of the crevasse, they cut the rope and tied it to a ski pole. They traversed around to the right to cross the crevasse and approached the accident site from below.

Hoffman stated that a large portion of the crevasse lip, approximately eight feet wide by four feet long and ten feet deep, had caved in. This volume of hard snow and ice was wedged into the crevasse as it tapered in at a point approximately 35 feet below the upper lip and 25 feet below the lower lip. The crevasse was ten feet wide at the top. Approximately two hours after Stump's fall, Max rappelled into the crevasse. He described the debris as a large volume of very hard and dense snow and ice about 15 feet deep. Large blocks were wedged into the crevasse. The climbing rope entered the debris from the top. There was no sign of Stump or the rope from beneath the debris. The crevasse was at least 60 feet deeper from the bottom of the debris. Max attempted to dig through the snow and ice and along the rope to find Stump, but without success. He pulled on the rope and yelled for Stump, but there was no response. Max and Hoffman felt that it was almost impossible for a person to survive such a fall and burial by the blocks and debris. Max felt that by digging further, he was in danger of loosening the blocks and being buried himself. Because of the perceived danger, their condition, the weather, and low probability of survival, Max and Hoffman decided to abandon their efforts to find Stump.

It was getting late in the day as Max and Hoffman continued their descent off the Ramp. In poor visibility, and dehydrated, frostbitten, and unsure of the route down from having lost their guide, they decided to camp for the night.

On May 22, Mark Bunker and Don Preiss, who were camped at 11,400 feet on the East Fork, heard distress calls from Max and Hoffman. At 0830 they began climbing up the Ramp and met Max and Hoffman at 12,600 feet. At 1300, Preiss reported the incident on CB radio to Gary Bocarde on the West Rib, who relayed the message to basecamp. Bunker and Preiss assisted Max and Hoffman in descending to camp at 11,400 feet.

At 1400, Ranger Jim Phillips and pilot Jim Hetton evacuated Max and Hoffman from 11,400 feet on the East Fork with the NPS Lama helicopter. Hoffman and Max had frostbite and were exhausted. The climbers showed Phillips the location of the accident at 14,700 feet on the Ramp. Hoffman and Max were then flown to basecamp and then to Talkeetna.

At 1435, Rangers Jim Phillips and Renny Jackson, in the NPS Lama helicopter, returned to the accident site at 14,700 feet on the Ramp. They observed the crevasse with Stump's climbing rope tied off to a ski pole above the crevasse. A large volume of debris with big chunks of snow and ice was wedged into the crevasse as Hoffman and Max had described. They hovered over the crevasse, looking for any sign of life. Due to the location and elevation of the nearest landing zone (16,000 feet), the fact that the incident occurred more than 25 hours earlier, and the exposure of rescuers to excessive hazards, a rescue/recovery effort was not initiated.

Stump's body remains buried on the mountain. Max was admitted to Humana Hospital in Anchorage for treatment of frostbite on both feet.

Analysis

This accident illustrates the hazards of climbing on glaciated terrain even for the most competent of mountaineers. Even when climbers are roped, crevasse falls can be fatal.

Slack rope between Stump and Max caused Stump to fall an excessive distance. A belay in this case would have provided a more secure rope system for stopping the fall. The size of crevasses on Alaska Range glaciers can be deceiving because of large overhanging lips. (Source: Jim Phillips, Mountaineering Ranger, Denali National Park)

FALL ON SNOW, INADEQUATE BELAY, WEATHER
Alaska, Mount McKinley

On May 17, 1992, the Canadian "GT-92" expedition departed from the Southeast Fork of the Kahiltna Glacier at 7,200 feet. They spent the next five days reaching the 14,000 foot camp. After spending five days there, they proceeded to 16,200 feet for one day. On May 29, they moved to 17,200 feet. On the 30th they attempted to summit, leaving camp at 1200. The weather at the time was very windy with winds coming from the northeast at 20-25 mph. The ambient temperature at the time of the departure was 0o F. The group proceeded to Denali Pass and apparently attempted the West Buttress route. They were observed below Arch Deacon's Tower at 18,700 feet by several groups at 1645. They appeared to have on all of their high altitude equipment, including face masks. The route was well wanded (100 feet between markers on the Football Field). The weather remained windy, estimated between 20 and 30 mph, with the ambient temperature still at 0o F. The group wasn't observed again until 2200, when they were seen by Gerald Guidroz, a member of the expedition "New World Order," descending the Summit Ridge at 20,000 feet. The weather at 17,200 feet had started to deteriorate, with the winds gusting up to 50 mph. Throughout the rest of the night, the weather continued to deteriorate, with winds at 17,200 feet in excess of 60 mph.

On the morning of May 31, Annie Duquette (Kahiltna basecamp manager) was notified by an expedition at 17,200 feet that the group "GT 92" had not yet returned from their summit attempt. Duquette informed the NPS Mountaineering Rangers in Talkeetna of the overdue expedition. The weather prevented an overflight of the summit area. At 1200, the weather cleared and an aerial search was launched at 1230. Ranger Roger Robinson and Pilot Cheri Fleming flew over the search area and spotted a group of four climbers roped together traversing around 19,200 feet on the Messner Coulior. This group was believed to be the Canadian Team "GT 92." The NPS patrol at 14,000 feet led by Ranger Daryl Miller was alerted by Robinson as to the whereabouts of the expedition, and Miller was able to locate the group with the use of binoculars. At 1437, Miller saw the rear climber in the group fall, dragging the other three members of the rope team down. They continued falling through the first rock band. The rope appeared to be severed. The expedition was still falling, even after a member had been separated from the rest of the group and was tumbling down the slope by himself after the rope was cut on the rocks. The group fell approximately 3,000 feet to 16,000 feet in the Messner Coulior.

About 1500, Billy Shott, Mike Abbott, Colin Grissom, and Ranger Daryl Miller, members of the NPS patrol at 14,000 feet, departed for the accident site. At 1735, they reached a backpack at 15,500 feet. Visibility was less than 25 feet with no visible sighting of the victims. Snow conditions on the slope were extremely unstable, and the patrol unanimously concurred that it was too unsafe to continue the search at the time. At 1822 they turned around.

On June 1 at 0700, Miller talked to South District Ranger J. D. Swed in Talkeetna and decided to make another rescue attempt. At 1025, Shott, Abbott, Grissom, and Miller left the 14,000 foot camp and progressed to the Messner Coulior. At 1305, the patrol arrived at the accident site where they discovered three bodies at 16,000 feet and one body at

16,200 feet separated from the rest of the group. The patrol concluded that the body at 16,200 feet would be too dangerous to reach due to unstable snow conditions. The bodies at 16,000 feet were laying on a slope of roughly 45 degrees in three feet of deep snow. Miller and his group spent 15 minutes at the accident site and then retreated. They found no personal identification but were able to confirm the identity of the four men through clothing descriptions given by other climbers. The patrol returned to camp by 1500, and Miller and Swed decided to attempt to retrieve the bodies using a helicopter with a long line and hook to eliminate the danger of exposing rescuers to potential avalanche conditions. On June 2, at 1100, the Lama successfully retrieved all four bodies and took them to 7,200 feet where pilot Cheri Fleming flew the bodies off the mountain to Talkeetna.

Analysis
The Canadian team chose to go to the summit in deteriorating weather, while other teams turned back. The conditions forced the Canadians to be exposed at the upper elevations to strong winds and cold temperatures for an extended period of time. Since the group had very little gear, this more than likely predisposed them to frostbite, hypothermia, dehydration, and acute mountain sickness. They most likely were traversing the upper part of the Messner Couloir to get out of the strong north winds. Due to the fact that they were all roped together with no intermediate protection, a single fall by one of the members caused the entire rope team to perish. (Source: Daryl Miller, Mountaineering Ranger, Denali National Park)

AVALANCHE, WEATHER
Alaska, Mount Foraker
On June 14, 1992, Tom Walter (34), Ritt Kellogg (28), and Colby Coombs (25) skied from the Southeast Fork of the Kahiltna Glacier to the base of the "Pink Panther" on the East Face of Mount Foraker. Approximately three inches of new snow fell on the evening and night of the 14th.

On the morning of the 15th, the weather cleared. Walter, Kellogg, and Coombs began climbing the lower one third of the route called the "S Couloir," a steep snow and ice couloir interspersed with rock bands. They camped at a level area at the base of a cornice ridge line on the top of this couloir. It snowed again that night.

On the morning of the 16th, they were unable to climb due to poor weather. Late in the day the weather cleared and they began climbing the cornice ridge which marks the middle third of the route. They climbed through the night, and completed this portion early on June 17. They arrived at the base of the final rock buttress, which marks the last third of the route, as the weather deteriorated. They dug a snow cave and bivouacked, waiting out the poor weather.

On June 18, the weather remained poor with additional snow accumulation. Early in the evening of the 18th the weather cleared. They began climbing the final rock buttress. The weather remained good until the final 300 feet, when it deteriorated with wind and poor visibility. They completed climbing the rock buttress and intended to stop and bivouac at the first opportunity. They continued to climb up the final 50 to 60 degree snow and ice slope above the rock buttress, anticipating a bivouac site at the crest of the Southeast Ridge about 13,500 feet.

At this time Walter was leading the rope team with Coombs in the middle and Kellogg at the end. There was 150 feet of rope between each, and they were ascending simultaneously at the same rate. They were not belaying. It is likely that no anchors were being used as running belay points.

Late that night, about one hour after topping out on the rock buttress and while climbing the upper portion of the final snow and ice slope at 13,100 feet, they were hit by an avalanche at a point approximately 400 feet below the crest of the ridge and 700 feet above the top of the rock buttress. As Coombs was hit with snow from above, he began to self-arrest with his ice axe. He was pushed downhill by avalanche debris for approximately 20 feet before being flipped over backwards and falling and tumbling out of control. Coombs was knocked unconscious and does not remember coming to a stop.

Early in the morning of the 19th, Coombs regained consciousness and found himself hanging by the climbing rope in the upper part of the rock buttress near 12,300 feet. Coombs was mentally oriented as to person and place, but disoriented as to time and purpose. He was experiencing pain over his entire body, and felt hypothermic. The climbing rope between Coombs and Walter was looped over a rock outcropping overhead, which prevented a much longer fall. Walter was hanging by the rope a short distance away, and Coombs was able to climb to him. Walter's face was covered with snow. Coombs cleared the airway and checked for a pulse, and determined that Walter was dead. Coombs removed a crampon and Walter's pack and clipped it into the slack rope between himself and Kellogg. During his efforts to escape from the rope system, Coombs cut the climbing rope between himself and Walter. Walter's body fell and slid out of sight into the rock buttress. Coombs then downclimbed a short distance to a small rock ledge, where he set up a double ice axe anchor and tied off Walter's pack. He yelled down attempting to contact Kellogg, but without success. Coombs then set up a bivouac on the ledge and attempted to rest for the remainder of the day and night.

On the morning of June 20, Coombs rappelled from his bivouac site approximately 130 feet down the rope between him and Kellogg and found Kellogg hanging upside down and tangled in the rope. Kellogg's face was covered with snow and he had no pulse. Large amounts of blood were streaked in the snow near his body. Coombs stated that it appeared obvious that Kellogg had died from multiple traumatic injuries. Kellogg fell an additional 20 feet as the climbing rope untangled itself while Coombs examined the body. Coombs descended the remainder of the rope, tied Kellogg to an ice axe anchor, and cut the climbing rope from Kellogg. He removed a tent and fuel from Kellogg's pack and reascended the rope back to his bivouac ledge. Coombs then traversed approximately 700 feet southeast and camped in a bergschrund near the crest of the Southeast Ridge.

On June 21, 22, and 23, Coombs descended the Southeast Ridge. The descent required numerous rappels, and unprotected downclimbing on steep slopes and through heavily crevassed areas. Coombs' progress was slow due to injuries sustained during his fall on the 18th. Late on June 23 he arrived at the base of the Pink Panther route, picked up extra equipment cached there, and began crossing the Kahiltna Glacier.

On June 24, about 0500, Coombs arrived at basecamp on the Southeast Fork of the Kahiltna Glacier. Exhausted, he camped in a tent left ten days earlier. At 1230 Coombs reported the incident to the Talkeetna Ranger Station via Basecamp Manager Annie Duquette. On June 25 at 0100, Coombs was examined by Ranger Jim Phillips. Coombs had pain in his neck, left shoulder, and left ankle. He was advised to minimize activity, have his left arm and ankle splinted, and fly directly from basecamp to Humana Hospital in Anchorage. Poor weather delayed evacuation for four days. Phillips reexamined Coombs and monitored his condition several times daily.

On June 28 at 0900, Coombs was flown to Talkeetna at his own expense by K2 Aviation. He was then transported by private vehicle to Humana Hospital and diagnosed as having a fractured cervical vertebrae, fractured left scapula, and a fractured left ankle.

Aerial searches on June 30 and July 1 revealed no further evidence or sign of Walter or Kellogg.

Analysis

Walter, Kellogg, and Coombs were each highly skilled mountaineers, with extensive Alaska Range experience. Although the Pink Panther route is considered a very difficult route by Alaska Range standards, Coombs stated that it was well within his team's technical ability. Coombs also stated that the climbers constantly reevaluated their situation and assessed the hazards, and felt that they were climbing conservatively. He does not know what he would have done differently.

The climbers ascended the route in three days, half the time required for the first ascent. They were climbing for long (approximately 20 hours) periods between rests. Although that is not unusual for fast and light alpine style ascents, fatigue may have been a contributing factor to the accident.

Deteriorating weather at the time of the accident created poor visibility to the point that Coombs was unable to see Walter 150 feet ahead. This may have prevented them from recognizing hazardous avalanche conditions.

The exact cause of the avalanche is unknown. Unsettled weather during the climb produced light to moderate snowfall amounts. At times winds were moderate to strong at high elevations. Potentially unstable snow conditions were present in some locations. The site was a broad, open snow and ice slope 50 degrees or steeper. Coombs stated that conditions were hard neve snow over ice, and that this surface did not and could not have slid. The avalanche was triggered at a location somewhere above Coombs. He speculates that either a loose snow avalanche sluffed down from above and hit the climbers, or Walter triggered a small, isolated slab avalanche. When the site was investigated from the air on July 1, there was no sign of a crown surface, cornice break, or any other signs of the avalanche.

Coombs was able to rule out a climbing fall as the cause of the accident. They were definitely hit by moving snow, which caused them to fall. On dangerous and exposed terrain they belayed or used running anchor points and climbed simultaneously. At the time of the accident, however, the terrain and conditions were perceived as not requiring belays or anchor points, and the team climbed simultaneously without anchor points. The use of running anchor points may have prevented the long fall which resulted from the avalanche. The evidence discovered at the scene on July 1 indicates that the climbing team fell at least 700 vertical feet. (Source: Jim Phillips, Mountaineering Ranger, Denali National Park)

FALL ON SNOW, SKI MOUNTAINEERING, EXCEEDING ABILITIES, INADEQUATE EQUIPMENT, BINDING ADJUSTMENT
Alaska, Chugach Mountains

From June 28 to July 5, 1992, I (Todd Miner, 36) was co-leading a University of Alaska Anchorage Wilderness Leadership Expedition. On the 5th, while skiing down the Raven Glacier, I fell, resulting in an injured knee. (Later diagnosed as a torn anterior cruciate ligament (ACL), torn medial collateral ligament, torn posterior cruciate ligament, dislocated patella, and damaged meniscus of the left knee.

It was the last day of an eight-day traverse of the Eklutna Glacier system. We had arisen at 0500, broken camp, and ascended 1700 feet to the Raven Headwall. It took us about three hours to get 15 people (13 class participants and two recreational climbers who met us at top) down the 600 foot high, 30 to 70 degree slope of the headwall. From there we had to ski down the Raven Glacier and then hike out the Crow Pass trail. The weather was warm (50° F), calm and we were in and out of a low hanging cloud with occasional rain.

The accident occurred about 1430 while we were skiing down the Raven Glacier, about half way between the Raven Headwall (where we accessed the glacier) and Crow Pass, where the glacier terminates. I was skiing in the rear on a two-person rope team, with a student. We were the lead rope team, roughly following an old ski trail, skiing large "S's" down an approximately 20 degree slope. Both of us had large packs (50-70 pounds) and old skins on our skis. I was also pulling a plastic sled with cord. I was skiing on Europa 99's with an older model Ramer binding.

While attempting to turn back to the right, I crossed my skis. I fell forward over my left knee. I screamed for Chip to help me as I immediately knew my knee was traumatized. I could not get up on my own due to the knee being stuck underneath me and to the large pack. Chip quickly came to my aid and helped me to sit up. When I looked at my knee I thought the patella was dislocated. The pain was intense, so in an attempt to relieve it, I asked Chip to slowly straighten out my leg. He did and I immediately felt, saw, and heard a pop; I assumed the patella had re-positioned itself. The pain level also immediately dropped, though it was still enough to make me nauseous. I got an ensolite pad underneath me and rested.

By this time the rest of the class had caught up. I was assisted with a sleeping bag around me, a hat, a pack to lean on, water (I was terribly thirsty), and lots of reassurance. Several students fashioned a splint out of a "Crazy Creek" chair, a piece of an ensolite pad, webbing, a cravat, and pack straps. Upon tightening of the splint, the pain was further reduced.

While the splint was being constructed, co-instructor David Cockerall was developing a rescue plan, conferring with our student "Leader of the Day," Ken Kibe, who is also a member of the Alaska Mountain Rescue group. Using our emergency aviation radio, student Jackson Fullbright established that radio communication was possible with passing airliners. I asked that I be given a chance to walk out before we tried a carry (or to sled me down) or call for a rescue.

I tried walking without a pack or sled and with the assistance of ski poles. My steps were tentative, but it was not too painful nor unstable so we gave it a try. The class distributed my gear amongst the other 12 members and with all of us on foot and roped we continued the descent. One and then two teams went ahead to scout the route. I could only take small steps but the snow surface was smooth and I could keep a steady pace. The further I went the less pain I felt. Every once in a while I would feel my knee start to buckle, but between the splint and the ski poles I was able to recover.

We decided to make the end of the glacier (or the start of the Crow Pass trail) the immediate goal. The only real difficult part was traversing a steep (45 degree) snow slope to get off the glacier. Thankfully, at this point, we ran into Scott Horacek and a party led by Diane Salee, folks who were hiking up the trail to meet us. They helped kick steps on the slope and to carry gear. Once on the trail the walking (limping) returned to being relatively easy for me. We regrouped at the U.S. Forest Service Crow Pass Cabin to see what our next move would be. I still felt like continuing on. Even if I hadn't felt like continuing, the "down to the deck" ceiling would have probably kept helicopters from getting in. In any event, it would have been hours before any kind of organized rescue could have gotten to us, so onward and downward I plodded.

Around 2030 I arrived at the trailhead along with a sweep crew. We loaded up the van and a pick-up truck and drove down to Girdwood. By the time we hit town it was too late to go to "FirstCare." We grabbed dinner and headed back to Anchorage. About 2330 assistant instructor Karen Pzeitmeir and I were dropped off at the emergency room at Providence Hospital. The knee had swollen considerably so diagnosis was apparently difficult. I was sent home some time after 0200, the doctor agreeing with my assumption that I had probably dislocated my patella.

Analysis
I believe the accident was the result of several contributing factors:

I am a poor, to at best mediocre, skier. One cannot learn if one does not fall. However, falling with a big pack in the back country does have risks.

I was having fun, perhaps too much fun. Contributing to this was my excitement at having gotten down the crux of the trip, the Headwall, and at being so close to the end of the trip. Hubris can be costly.

The binding was set too tight. We had exchanged bindings just before the trip and even though I knew my bindings had been tightened considerably, I did not take the time to re-loosen them. It is no wonder they did not release. This was the main contributing factor to the injury.

Perhaps I wouldn't have fallen if I hadn't been roped. (The rope was a distraction.) Maybe this is a case where going unroped would have been a safer alternative than roping through the very few crevasses. (Source: Todd A. Miner)

AVALANCHE, PARTY SEPARATED—NO RESCUE ATTEMPT
Alaska, Flattop Mountain
In October of 1992, four Anchorage climbers were ascending a gully on Flattop Mountain just outside of Anchorage when they were struck by an avalanche. Two were buried, one popped out, and one escaped being hit. The latter two descended.

When rescuers returned a few hours later, they found one victim quickly. He was wearing a beacon. The other was located after finding his ski pole just barely sticking out of the snow. Both victims had succumbed.

Analysis
It is not known why the two survivors made no attempt to locate the two victims. It is known that one of them, Dave Hart, was on Mount McKinley in the spring, and while descending from the summit, separated from his partner who was not doing well. Hart descended on his own, while his partner required rescue, which was accomplished by a guided party nearby. (Source: Alaskan climbers)

FALL ON ROCK, FOOTHOLD BROKE OFF, CLIMBING UNROPED
Arizona, Cochise Stronghold, Rockfellow Dome
On November 26, 1992, my friends and I (45) were checking out the climbs on Rockfellow Dome with the intention of climbing there the next day. At the base of the dome is a scree of large, smooth granite boulders. To return to camp, we had to climb over one such boul-

der. To the right of the rock on which I was standing and three feet up was a granite flake. I followed a friend, who used the flake as a foothold. Because I am much heavier than she, I first tried to test the flake by kicking it. It seemed stable, but when my full weight had shifted up and right, it broke. The crystals I gripped with my fingers were inadequate to keep me from falling. I missed the rock from which I had stepped up and landed in a crevasse (*sic*) 15 feet below. My pelvis and both arms were broken. The ulna of my right arm was protruding through the skin

I don't remember landing or being extracted from the crevasse (*sic*). At first I was confused. Two rescue teams eventually arrived to help but they could not carry me over the rugged terrain, especially at night. Eventually an Air Force helicopter flew from the other end of the state, reaching us at 0130, ten hours after my fall. The helicopter had to hover within a few yards of the dome and winch me up. I was spinning wildly at the end of the cable. We flew to Tucson but landed at the wrong hospital. I completed the journey in an ambulance.

Analysis
I will never trust a flake. If I had been roped up and following I would not have been hurt. Lacking the rope, I would seek another route.

Always carry drugs! The medics who came to the rescue did not have any. If my friends had not brought codeine with them, I would have had to do with out pain killers until I reached the hospital. (Source: Barbara Calef)

FALL ON ROCK, PLACED INADEQUATE PROTECTION
California, Joshua Tree National Monument
On January 31, 1992, at 1450, Laurie Lauer (32) fell near the top of White Lightning (5.7). Due to the stretch in the rope and the distance from her last piece of protection, the distance of the fall was 15 to 20 feet. She landed on a slab, resulting in a fractured lower right leg. She was evacuated by park rangers. (Source: David Trevino, Ranger, Joshua Tree National Monument)

FALL ON ROCK, PLACED INADEQUATE PROTECTION
California, Joshua Tree National Monument
On February 1, 1992, Michael Gardiner (31) fell while leading the Hobbit Roof (5.10). Gardiner's top piece of protection, a #2 Friend, pulled out, so he fell 30 feet to the ground. He landed on his feet, then fell to his side, hitting his head against the rock. He sustained a broken nose and sore jaw.

Analysis
Where Gardiner fell is 5.9. He was relying on only one piece of protection. He was very lucky not to have sustained greater injury, as the landing area is not good. (Source: Debbie Brenchley, Ranger, Joshua Tree National Monument)

FALL ON ROCK, OFF ROUTE, UNPLANNED BIVOUAC, MISUNDERSTANDING OF RATING SYSTEM, INADEQUATE EQUIPMENT
Arizona, Canyon Spring Wall, De Grazia
The purpose of the trip (on December 2, 1992) was to complete a multi-pitch climb. De Grazia was selected because it provided good "exposure" with moderate difficulty. The

description in the guide book led us to believe that the third pitch was the most difficult and the only pitch rated 5.7 followed by two pitches of lesser difficulty.

We left home an hour off schedule and the approach took an hour more than planned. We ate a quick lunch and began climbing around 1130. After finishing the third pitch, we estimated the sun would set in a few hours. We decided to continue up expecting the last two pitches would not take as long as the third pitch. The lead climber (27) went off route, but was able to traverse left gaining the belay station. By the time the second climber (31) reached that belay point, the sun had set. The lead climber continued up, unintentionally going off route to gain a ledge. When the second climber reached the ledge, it was decided it was too dark to continue.

The ledge led up to a large flake which created a crevasse providing shelter. We secured our position in the crevasse and took measures to protect us against hypothermia.

The following morning when it was light enough to see, we prepared to climb again. At this time a truck, presumably from the Arizona Mountaineering Club, arrived and sounded a siren. We made no contact with him and started to climb at 0730. The leader climbed up approximately 15 feet, clipping into existing webbing and then moving right out of the crevasse and onto a small ledge. He continued up the face and began moving left into the crack when he fell. He fell approximately ten feet to a ledge, landing on his feet. He continued down clearing the crevasse and landed on his back on the ledge just below the belayer—a total fall of about 30 feet.

After assessing injuries, we called down to the truck for help, communicating the need for help. He told us help is on its way. In a few hours several vehicles and a rescue helicopter arrived.

We had some difficulty signaling the helicopter, but after several passes we were located. Around 1430 the paramedic had descended from the top to our position.

Tom attended to my injuries, immobilizing my right ankle. By this time we were fairly dehydrated and the paramedic gave us some water and a little food. Tom coordinated how my partner and I would ascend with the rest of the rescue team above. An hour or so had passed and then the haul system was ready. I was fitted with a helmet and chest harness and was slowly hauled to the top of the rock. Once I reached the location of the haul system, I was escorted to where the helicopter could land and pick me up (approximately 50 yards). The helicopter landed once I was in position and flew me down to the parking area. At this same time my partner was being hauled to the top. I was escorted to the ambulance and was checked over for injuries. When Phil had come to the parking area, I refused the ambulance ride to the hospital, since my injuries were not life threatening.

After returning home I had my wife take me to a clinic for x-rays and treatment. Two small fractures to the lower tibula, just above the right ankle.

Analysis

I have learned that a 5.7 in Arizona is equal to a 5.9 in Yosemite. Previously I thought the Yosemite Decimal System would transfer to other places equally. I was told the day of the rescue by several people that Arizona doesn't rate their climbs the same as Yosemite, which I'm used to. On future multi-pitch climbs, I will bring two ropes giving me the option to rappel if I lack sufficient daylight to finish the climb. (Source: Will Wakeling)

FALLING ROCK Arizona, Flagstaff, Priest Draw ON February 21, 1992, Robert Drysdale (22) was killed when a large block was dislodged from the top of a boulder problem and hit him in the back of the head. Drysdale, originally from Scotland, was a very experienced climber, having started at age 15. He established many difficult climbs, often without much protection. (Source: Magazine and newspaper clips)

(Editor's Note: Angelo Kokenakis, from Flagstaff, also reported a fatality from lightning on Mount Humphreys. While this was a hiking accident, it is important for climbers new to the area to know that lightning is common here in the afternoon.)

STRANDED, EXCEEDING ABILITIES, INADEQUATE PROTECTION
California, Yosemite Valley, Swan Slab

On April 27, 1992, at 1430, Karen Hoeppner telephoned NPS dispatch and reported that James Dziadulewicz had fallen while rock climbing on Swan Slab, and was injured on a ledge approximately 30 feet above the ground. I responded with Ranger Obernesser, picked up Hoeppner and located Dziadulewicz at 1440.

Dziadulewicz was on a ledge approximately 30 vertical feet above the ground. He was in a stable position, and said that he had injured his leg and scraped his hands. I assumed incident command while Ranger Obernesser climbed to Dziadulewicz and led the medical team. Ranger Ray arrived with a technical rescue team and supervised the technical rescue, in which Dziadulewicz was immobilized in a litter and lowered to the ground. Rescuers climbing to Dziadulewicz were required to be on belay or ascend a fixed rope due to the steep, exposed rock face, and rescuers were exposed to falling rock several times during the rescue. Dziadulewicz was transported to the Yosemite Medical Clinic, where he was diagnosed as having a fractured left tibia and severe abrasions to both hands and forearms.

Analysis

At 1435 I interviewed Hoeppner at the accident scene. Hoeppner said that Dziadulewicz had been demonstrating basic rock climbing to her. She said that he had rappelled approximately 40 vertical feet down a rock face and was trying to climb back up when he fell. Hoeppner said she was not sure why he fell.

At 1630 I interviewed Dziadulewicz at the Yosemite Medical Clinic. He learned to climb from a friend and has never had any formal training. He said that approximately ten years ago, he rappelled a lot, and that he now climbs approximately ten times a year. He said the hardest routes he has ever climbed were following 5.8, and said he had only done that three or four times. Dziadulewicz said he has climbed in Yosemite a few times, but has never climbed on Swan Slab before. He had not done any significant routes in Yosemite, but had just "messed around" at the base of climbs that friends were doing. He didn't have jumars with him and did not know what a prusik is.

Dziadulewicz described himself as a person who isn't afraid of trying anything, and said he tends to "just go ahead and do it" without a lot of thought. He said he sometimes gets a little crazy and "goes to extremes," and said he thought he'd gone too far today. He also said, "I'm not all that crazy about heights." He said that he was hurrying to show her as much as possible about climbing in the short time they had left in Yosemite before leaving later in the day for southern California. He also said that he was trying to show off a little bit to impress Hoeppner with how easy climbing is and how much he knows about it.

He said he had just rappelled down a rock face approximately 40 feet (immediately above the ledge where he was found) and wanted to climb back up to show Hoeppner how to rappel. He said he saw an easy and apparently safe route up a chimney a short distance to the west, but said he didn't feel like going out of his way because he was "feeling lazy." Dziadulewicz said he decided to just climb back up his rappel rope, to show Hoeppner how easy it was. He said he clipped a carabiner to his harness and then clipped it around the rope, but realized that the freely-sliding carabiner provided no safety. Dziadulewicz said he climbed hand-over-hand back up to his rappel rope, but near the top, the rope was tight against the rock and he couldn't get a grip on it. He said he then tried to descend hand-over-hand back down the rope, but part way down he tired and couldn't continue, and his hands began to slide down the rope. Dziadulewicz said that after sliding approximately five feet, he let go, and slid uncontrollably the rest of the way down the face. He said he realized at the time that what he was doing was not the safest way to climb, but thought he could get away with it.

I cited Dziadulewicz for 36 CFR 2.34a4 (Disorderly Conduct— Creating a Hazardous Condition) with a mandatory court appearance. I recommended that Dziadulewicz make restitution for the $633.41 rescue cost to the Yosemite Mountain Safety Fund. (Source: David A. Brennan, SAR Ranger, Yosemite National Park)

FALL ON ROCK, ASCENDERS DETACHED FROM ROPE
California, Yosemite Valley, El Capitan

On May 12, 1992, John McDonald (31) was cleaning an aid pitch on the Zodiac route (VI, 5.11, A3) on El Capitan, when his ascenders apparently became detached from his rope and he fell about 100 feet to the end of the rope. He suffered serious rope burns to his hands and had to stop the climb, but he was able to ascend a rope lowered from the summit by NPS rescuers. I interviewed him about the accident the following day and also on December 12.

McDonald stated to me, in essence, the following: At the time of his accident, McDonald had been rock climbing regularly for six years. He had climbed three Grade V walls and one Grade VI (the Nose on El Capitan). His partner at the time of the accident, Fred Berman, had five years of climbing experience, including one Grade VI (the Regular Northwest Face of Half Dome). They fixed the first three pitches of the Zodiac on Friday, May 8, and started up for good on Sunday, climbing about three pitches per day with no problems.

On Tuesday morning Berman led the tenth, "Nipple," pitch and hauled the bag while McDonald cleaned. McDonald climbed the 11 mm rope with two CMI Ultrascenders rigged in standard wall fashion, i.e., an *etrier* from each ascender to a foot and a daisy chain from each ascender to his seat harness. The left ascender was the upper one. The daisy chains were just snug at full reach and did not impair the positioning or function of the ascenders.

In addition to staying tied to his end of the rope, McDonald made a habit of tying in "short" as he ascended, to prevent a long fall if something went wrong. He tied to the rope just below his ascenders, with a clove hitch to a locking carabiner on his harness. As he climbed, he repeated the process whenever the loop of slack growing below him became dangerously long. He last tied in short just below the Nipple, and when he arrived at the final placement on the pitch, about 75 feet of slack rope hung beneath him. The last placement was a fixed piton with a single carabiner. From that carabiner the rope slanted up left at about 35-40 degrees from the vertical, to the belay five or six feet away.

McDonald saw that the carabiner's gate was against the wall, and that the sideways tension on the carabiner (from his weight on the rope below it, plus the change in direction of the rope) would make it difficult to unclip the rope. So he passed his upper (left) ascender around the carabiner, to put all his weight above it. He had a hard time reattaching the ascender to the rope. First, a bulge in the wall above the placement, plus his own weight still on the rope below the carabiner, held the rope tight against the rock. Second, having to reach above and to the left put his wrist at an awkward angle as he tried to scoop the rope into the channel of the ascender.

He felt that he had reattached the ascender properly, but it was hard to tell from his position, and the tension in the rope held the ascender tightly against the rock. He pushed it up the rope to get the slack out of the daisy chain, and looked at it. He doesn't remember being able to see the position of the cam or the safety lever, but the ascender appeared to be oriented correctly, i.e., with the frame parallel to the rope, so he didn't check it after that.

McDonald felt they were a little behind schedule so he was trying to clean as fast as possible. He was also feeling a bit bold, the wall was steep (nothing to hit, if he fell), and "the belay was right there." So while he was aware of the big loop of slack, and while normally he might have tied in short again, he decided not to take the time—he would just go for it. If he just weighted the upper ascender, McDonald felt he would swing out of reach of the piton, so he gripped the rope above the carabiner with his left hand, taking some of his weight, hoping to keep himself near the piece. As he did so, he heard a click in the upper ascender and assumed that was the cam engaging.

He does not remember what, if anything, he did with the carabiner or the lower ascender at that time. The next thing he does know is that he suddenly began to fall. He gripped the rope with both hands, but he was unable to stop himself and the pain from the friction of the rope made him let go. He fell to the end of the rope, probably 100 feet including rope stretch. He hit nothing along the way and, other than his hands, was not hurt.

Full of adrenaline from the experience, he managed to re-rig and get up the rope to the belay. The palmar surfaces of several fingers on each hand were badly abraded, so he covered them with Neosporin and tape. He didn't feel he could continue climbing, and rappelling seemed too difficult under the circumstances, so he and Berman yelled to a party at the base of the wall who contacted the Park Service. A rescue team flew to the summit and lowered a rescuer to them. McDonald was able to slowly climb the rescuer's rope 700 feet to the top under his own power. With medical care, his hands have fully recovered.

Analysis
McDonald does not remember whether the ascenders were on the rope after the fall. However, it seems likely they weren't, for the following reasons: First, if he had been gripping the ascenders and holding the cams open, he would not have burned his hands, and if he had let go, the ascenders would have grabbed the rope, stopping the fall and/or possibly tearing the rope. Second, if the cams had been locked partially open, a brief contact with the rope during the fall might have been enough for them to unlock and grab the rope. We have not tested this possibility.

After the incident the rope showed no obvious surface damage. The ascenders—previously used only on the climbs mentioned above—appeared to be in good working condition. No rope fibers were caught in them, although their use during the rescue may have cleaned them. McDonald does not remember removing the lower ascender before the fall, but he guesses that he may have done so to keep it from jamming against the carabiner as he swung to the left. He also does not remember cleaning the placement (unclipping the carabiner from the rope and from the piton), but he is sure he was able to climb directly to the belay, after the fall, without cleaning anything. So he thinks he may have supported his weight partially with the upper ascender and partially with his left hand long enough to remove the lower ascender and to unclip the carabiner, before the fall.

Despite McDonald's attempt to check the upper ascender after moving it past the carabiner, it may have been sufficiently locked onto the rope. Possibly the rock caught and opened the safety lever as he pushed the ascender upward—he does not remember if the ascender was sticking out from the rock or laying flat against it. (I did not have an Ultrascender with which to test this possibility. However, I was able to get a Jumar to release the rope, by pushing it upward while its "open," or "rope entry," side was pressed flat against the rock. Rough spots on the wall caught the safety lever and held it back as I pushed the ascender upward, and pressure from the rope opened the cam. Since conditions had to be just right, I can't estimate the probability of this happening in the field, and this characteristic does not necessarily hold true for the Ultrascender.)

McDonald stated that the Ultrascender can lock half-way open, when the cam catches on the first notch. He feels this is what led to the ascender coming off the rope. He has looked at other brands and feels that they don't do that. Other than the test suggestions mentioned above, I have not tested this claim.

Suggestions to climbers (these may not apply in all situations):

Get to know your ascenders. Know the correct rope diameters to use. Be able to tell, by look and feel, when the ascenders are on the rope correctly. According to CMI, for example, you can feel the position of the safety lever of the Ultrascender when you grip the handle.

Make sure the rest of the rigging allows the ascenders to function properly. At least one death may have occurred when a too-short daisy chain prevented an ascender cam and its safety from locking onto the rope. (Schrattner, Yosemite, 9/24/87. The report is condensed in *Accidents in North American Mountaineering, AAC, 1988*, p. 36.)

Usually you do not need to completely remove the lower ascender from the rope when cleaning a traverse. With the right timing, you can open the cam of the lower ascender as your weight shifts to the upper one. (The safety is still engaged, so the rope won't come out.) As you swing under the next piece, the rope will move through the lower ascender without jamming it into the piece to be cleaned. This method is fast and it keeps both ascenders on the rope. It is a bit dynamic, however, so I'm not sure I'd try it on a row of A4 placements!

The best insurance is to tie in short, any time you get into an awkward situation, e.g., cleaning a traverse. Do it even when there is nothing to hit in a long fall—there's no sense in stressing—or breaking—your gear. (Source: John Dill, SAR Ranger, Yosemite National Park)

FALL ON ROCK, PLACED NO PROTECTION
California, Yosemite Valley, El Capitan

On May 16, 1992, while climbing the second pitch of "The Nose" route on El Capitan, Bruce Burns (37) fell about 60 feet while leading. He was injured, and was unconscious for a short period of time. His partners lowered him to the bottom of the third pitch, to within 200 feet above the ground on third and fourth class rock. From there he was rescued by an NPS team.

Analysis
After the completion of his medical treatment, I interviewed Burns at the Yosemite Medical Clinic. He and his climbing partners, Shane Stewart and Phillip Cobbin, stated, in essence, that Burns was leading belayed by Stewart. Burns was stemming up a corner about 25 feet above the belay station when he tried to reach a long, tied off sling that protects the next section when his right foot slipped off, causing a fall. (The area where he fell is rated approximately 5.9). Burns had placed no protection above the belay station bolts. He fell feet first about 30 feet until hitting a rock projection with his left foot, which flipped him over head first. He fell about 30 feet more head down, impacting his shoulder, thigh and the back of his head before being stopped by Stewart's belay. Stewart and Cobbin reported that after his fall, Burns was hanging upside down on the rope and was unconscious and unresponsive for approximately one minute. Stewart lowered Burns to the bottom of the first pitch. Stewart and Cobbin yelled for help, and bystanders left to report the accident.

Stewart and Burns stated that they have climbed "The Nose" route together six times in the past. Burns has been a climber since 1980, and has climbed numerous free and aid routes both in Yosemite and elsewhere up to the level of 5.11c and A3. Burns, Stewart and Cobbin agreed that the accident could possibly have been prevented or its seriousness reduced if Burns had placed protection between the belay and the place where he fell from. (Source: Daniel Horner, Ranger, Yosemite National Park)

FALL ON ROCK, FATIGUE, LOSS OF CONCENTRATION
California, Yosemite Valley, Cathedral Spires
On the evening of May 27, 1992, the park received a report of an accident on Higher Cathedral Rock. The reporting party had been on the Cathedral Spires at 1800 when they heard yells for help from Higher Rock. They said the climbers in trouble were reporting a person with a broken leg on the route Braille Book. It took the reporting party until 2200 to descend and make the report of the accident to the NPS.

The Valley District night shift rangers organized an initial response consisting of four persons. They hiked up Spires Gully in the dark and were able to make verbal contact with the injured party about midnight. They continued up, and between 0400 and 0500, ranger Mike Ray was able to rappel from the top to the victim's location on the route. He stabilized the victim's lower leg with an air splint.

The park helicopter was able to lower a Stokes litter. The victim was placed in the litter and then he was short hauled under the helicopter to El Capitan meadow. He was then driven by NPS vehicle to the Yosemite Medical Clinic where he was treated for a comminuted fracture of the lower leg.

Analysis
Jurek Kopacz (47) is a very experienced mountaineer from Poland. He has climbed for 25 years, including routes in the Andes, Alaska, the Alps, and several big wall routes in Yosemite Valley. He describes himself as able to lead 5.9 to 5.10 rock climbing leader.

Kopacz had led the entire climb of Braille Book before the accident. Around 1800 he was leading what was their eighth pitch of the day, near the end of the climb. He was traversing to his right, to what is described in the Roper guide as the "improbable crack" which leads to the large pine tree near the top of the Sequel route. He was doing a friction move, which he estimates was about 5.4, and was about one foot from reaching the crack. After that, he said, the climbing would have become very easy. He said he was about four feet above, and ten to 12 feet to the right of his last piece of protection. He stated he could have easily climbed a little higher and placed another piece to protect the traverse. However, the climbing was easy, Kopacz was anxious to get off the climb, and he stated that, "I wanted to be in the Valley drinking beer." Due to these reasons, he said, "I did not have much concentration." Kopacz further told me that he was very tired, and that he was not wearing his "good" climbing shoes because they were being resoled. He felt these factors also contributed to the fall. However, he added that there was no excuse, the cause of the accident was mental mistakes. (Source: Daniel Horner, Ranger, Yosemite National Park)

FALL ON ROCK—ROCK FOOTHOLD BROKE OFF, PROTECTION PULLED OUT, NO HARD HAT
California, Joshua Tree National Monument
On June 7, 1992, William Oliver (30) was leading Beck's Bet (5.5). He was about 25 feet up the route, just past his second piece of protection, when the rock knob he had stepped onto broke off. He fell, his protection pulled out, and he landed on his belayer. Oliver went unconscious briefly. His partner sustained a bruised thigh and lacerated ankle. They were both evacuated to medical facilities, examined, treated and released that evening. (Source: Kip Knapp, Ranger, Joshua Tree National Monument)

Analysis
Bill Oliver wrote an article about his accident for the Southern California Mountaineering Association newsletter, and sent it along to ANAM. In his own words:

> I always, always wear (my hard hat) when climbing—even though virtually no one else does and it looks totally uncool. Today, needless to say, I had inadvertently left it in the car and I didn't bother to go back and get it once we got to the wall... Since there's no guarantee against an unexpected fall, it behooves climbers to carry adequate medical insurance—and the use of a hard hat might not be totally uncool.

The total charge for his ambulance ride and hospital—including the CAT scan—came to $6,251!

STRANDED, INADEQUATE EQUIPMENT AND CLOTHING, WEATHER
California, Yosemite National Park, Stately Pleasure Dome
On June 24, 1992, Anne Tuite (21) and Sean Costello (29) became stranded on Stately Pleasure Dome due to a rain and hail storm.

After a difficult rescue in the storm, Tuite was flown off the dome at 2040 and transported to medical facilities where she was treated for mild to moderate hypothermia. Costello and the rescue rangers rappelled off. (Source: Dave Page, Ranger, Yosemite National Park)

Analysis
Costello and Tuite became stranded because of the weather. They chose to continue climbing as they only had one rope and could not rappel. A contributing factor was their lack of warm clothing and rain gear. Both climbers were from Ireland. Costello was apparently fairly experienced; Tuite was a novice. They took only one rope, no headlamps or

storm clothes because they thought they'd get off in time. They realized they'd made a potentially serious mistake. They were not cited for negligence, but, in the future, climbers in similar situations may be. (Source: John Dill, SAR Ranger, Yosemite National Park)

FALL ON ROCK, PROTECTION PULLED OUT
California, Tahquitz Rock, Consolation

On July 4, 1992, I was about 25 feet into the third pitch of our climb when I came off. Two pieces that I had placed failed. One was a small Metolius tri-cam unit a few feet below the spot from which I fell. The cams tipped out and reversed. A foot or two below that piece I had a wired, curved stopper or rock. It didn't wind up in front of my harness afterward. One is left to guess what happened to it. Perhaps the carabiner failed or the swage on the piece failed. Mike Jaffe remembers hearing two distinct sounds just before I flew past. He describes it as, "Bam! Bam!" The first sound was likely the TCU blowing out, the second the other piece. In any case, I went on a longer ride than expected. I think it was good fortune that I had just cleared an overhang, so I took to the air and didn't go tumbling down. I have a vague recollection of wondering what had happened with my pieces and when I was going to stop falling. I had no sense that I was going to die, no life flashing before my eyes, just gray and blue and then some green. When I finally stopped falling and got some friction underfoot, on a small face and held by the rope, I was fairly calm. I talked with Mike, letting him know I was OK but for some pain in my right knee. Very little in the way of abrasions and blood. He let me know that he had hurt his hands, one badly. I asked him to let me down a bit so I could move over into a crack. I clipped into a fixed piece there so that we could be somewhat more free to get our bearings on the situation. I considered climbing up to him and going up and off by a different route. On testing my right knee it became apparent that I wouldn't be doing any more climbing that day. Mike said he didn't think he would be able to climb either, given the injuries to his hands. We went about rappelling down the roughly 350 feet to the base. This took an hour because of our various infirmities, the perceived need to deal with the damage to the rope (discovered only after I almost rappelled past the worst of the damaged spots), and our somewhat unsettled, not totally clear state of mind.

The piece that finally held my fall was a small, solid hex slung on perlon, a good placement just right and above the place where Mike sat on belay. When he caught me he was pulled over into the piece. Some rope ran through his hands and the belay device (a new Black Diamond figure eight with red anodizing), burned his hands in the process. As a medical student, Mike was impressed with the fact that, although the burn when through the dermis and some blood vessels, there was little bleeding because the wounds were instantaneously cauterized. (Source: From a letter sent to New England Ropes and ANAM by Terry Hartig)

(Editor's Note: Hartig was impressed by the fact that his 60 foot leader fall did not result in the rope parting. We were impressed by the lack of more serious injuries.)

FALLING ROCK
California, Yosemite Valley, Leaning Tower

On July 5, 1992, I spoke with Brad Young (32) at the Yosemite Medical Clinic about a climbing accident that he and his climbing partner Doug Burton (age not noted) were involved in on the Leaning Tower.

Young told me that they started on the climb from the Bridalveil Parking Lot at 0900. They walked from the lot and arrived at the base of the climb at 1230. Young led the first and fourth pitches as described in the climbing book. Burton led the second and third pitches as one. Young said that he had done the regular route before. They arrived at the Ahwahnee Ledge between 1930 and 2000 and spent the night there.

On July 4, Young started the A-4 pitch at 0815. He finished the pitch about 1000. Burton started the next pitch about 1115 after sorting the gear. It was during the climb of this pitch, A-3, that Burton took a 15 foot fall. He was not injured and continued the climb. He finished the pitch about 1500. Young said it took a while because Burton was not as experienced. Young came up to Burton and re-racked the gear. He then began the third to the last pitch. He was about 20 feet up in the climb when he came upon a flake on the right. He said it looked like an obvious place to go. He mentioned that it was a thin flake but it was tucked behind another flake so he thought it would not be a problem. The flake was almost three feet off to the right of Burton. Young said that he did not warn Burton that he was testing the flake. He thought that if it fell it would miss Burton as there was a three foot space. Young put in a #1 Friend and clipped in his daisy chain to the Friend. He pulled on it and the flake came off. He yelled, "Rock," immediately. The flake fell to the left and not to the right as expected. Young said that the flake fell to the left because of the fracture line. When he yelled rock, Burton looked up and the flake struck him on the forehead. Fortunately, Burton was wearing a helmet.

The force of the blow caused Burton to become unconscious. Young said that Burton was bleeding from the forehead. He downclimbed immediately. He thought Burton was dead. He had some difficulty in downclimbing as he had to climb through the system already rigged. When he was downclimbing and got along side of Burton, Young said that he was yelling, trying to get a response from him. After about five minutes he said that he detected a moaning sound. Young said that he gave him a brief check and determined that the head wound was the most serious. He checked his fingers and toes and asked him about pain in his neck. Burton was coming around and could speak. Young removed the helmet and bandaged up the head wound and replaced the helmet. He then secured Burton on the wall.

Young then downclimbed and brought up the portaledge. He set it up and transferred Burton from the hammock to the portaledge. He placed Burton in his jacket and sleeping bag. He checked the pupils in his eyes. At this time he felt that Burton was improving. Burton told Young that he was allergic to penicillin and morphine. Young kept talking to Burton and rechecking him. He yelled for help and reported his situation to visitors below. Rescuers soon arrived. (Source: Daniel Horner, Ranger, Yosemite National Park)

(Editor's Note: Ranger John Dill sent a sketch of the helmet. He noted that the rock had split the shell, the suspension, his scalp and his skull—but not the meninges. As Dill put it, "Send the boy to Vegas—with my money!")

FALL ON ROCK, INADEQUATE PROTECTION, INADEQUATE BELAY, EXCEEDING ABILITIES
California, Yosemite Valley, Bishops Terrace
Keith Kramer (22) was planning on climbing Bishops Terrace with a new climbing partner who had little to no experience. Kramer did not have a guide book and was able

to locate Bishops Terrace. Kramer only had a short period of time to climb that afternoon, as he was expected at work at 1530. While looking for the Terrace, Kramer came across Serenity Crack. He stated: "I was running out of time and wanted to climb badly. The crack looked fairly easy to I decided to try it. I climbed up to the first bolt and then came back down because none of my pro would fit. I was running out of time to climb so I said the hell with it and started climbing again. I clipped the first bolt and was almost to the second, within five inches, when my feet started to slip. I yelled for my partner to catch me as I started to slide down on my knees and hands. I could see my partner below me all ready to catch me, but I hit the ground before the rope tightened up." Kramer's partner, Alan Carrey, ran for help to the Ahwahnee where he phoned 911. Kramer was evacuated by park rangers. He had sustained a closed fracture of the tibula and fibula. (Source: John Dill, SAR Ranger, Yosemite National Park)

STRANDED, INADEQUATE CLOTHING, WEATHER
California, Yosemite National Park, Stately Pleasure Dome
On July 14, 1992, Gary Damsley (23) and Allyson Pendleton (29) became stranded during a rain storm they experienced one pitch from the top of South Crack. They became too cold to climb and had to be rescued. (Source: Fred Koegler, Ranger, Yosemite National Park)

Analysis
They did not have warm clothing or rain gear with them, and were not aware of the changing weather. This incident nearly parallels the one reported on June 24, only these climbers are from California, not Ireland, and so might have been expected to be more aware of potential weather conditions. (Source: Jed Williamson)

FALL ON ROCK, NO SPOTTER
California, Yosemite Valley, Swan Slab
On July 23, 1992, Michael Poulin fell about eight feet to the ground while bouldering in the Swan Slab area. He sustained a severely angulated right ankle fracture. (Source: C. Jacobi, Ranger, Yosemite National Park)

(Editor's Note: Many injuries could be prevented if proper spotting techniques were used while bouldering—provided the climber is no more than six or eight feet above the spotter.)

FALL TO GROUND ON RAPPEL, INADEQUATE BELAY, NO HARD HAT
California, Yosemite National Park, Puppy Dome
On July 24, 1992, Mike James (22) and his fellow counselor from a Seventh Day Adventist Camp (Camp Wawona) had set up a rappel on "Do or Fly," an overhanging climb on Puppy Dome. The intent was to teach students to trust each other by having one student rappel "hands-off" (no attempt to brake) while a second student, at the bottom, stops the rappeller by pulling on the rope. James rappelled, but was not stopped before hitting the ground head first. The tension on the rope then bungied him back up, suspending him off the ground. He was evacuated by ranger to Yosemite Medical Clinic.

Analysis
Interviews with the victim's party revealed that they were rappelling young members of the group on dynamic rope, allowing them to "bounce" on the stretch of the rope. James was rappelling and the person maintaining tension with a belay device neglected to compensate for the difference in weight between James' adult stature and that of the students'. James fell, the stretch in the rope allowing him to strike the talus at the base of the wall. James was not wearing a helmet at the time of the fall, supposedly because there were not enough for the group, although not all of the group were at the summit or participating at the base in any fashion so as to require a helmet. (Source: K. L. O'Connor-Henry, Ranger, Yosemite National Park)

(Editor's Note: Here is an example of a school/camp using climbing as a vehicle for personal growth. While we must count such incidents as part of the climbing accident data, it should be noted that the individuals involved are not climbers.)

FALL ON ICE, PLACED NO PROTECTION, EXCEEDING ABILITIES
California, Dana Glacier
On July 26, 1992, at 1515 Ranger Dave Page received a report of a climbing accident on the Dana Glacier. The reporting party, Robert Gordon, was at the Tioga Pass Entrance Station. Gordon indicated that two individuals climbing above him on the Dana Glacier had taken a 500 foot fall and that one of the individuals was seriously injured. Dana Glacier is outside the park boundary and Mono County Sheriff was called and notified of the incident. At that time I informed Sargent Cole Hampton that the park helicopter and personnel were available to respond if Mono County requested our assistance. Sargent Cole requested that we respond and asked that we keep him informed of what was happening.

Richard Vance was leading the climb up the ice gully on the Dana Glacier when his climbing partner, Joel Johnson, lost his footing and fell. Vance and Johnson were roped together and Vance had not put in any protection. Vance had no ice protection, only rock protection which he felt was useless in the rocks at the sides of the gully. Johnson gave no warning when he fell and pulled Vance down with him. Vance made an attempt at self-arrest but it was useless on the ice. Both climbers fell approximately 500 feet clearing the bergschrund in the process. Vance and Johnson came to rest on mixed snow and talus at approximately 11,700 feet. Vance was uninjured and indicated that Johnson had lost consciousness for about one minute and he remained disoriented for approximately ten minutes. Vance placed Johnson on a thermarest pad and put a sleeping bag over him to keep him warm. Both climbers were wearing helmets; however, Vance lost his during the fall. Robert Gordon, who was climbing below Vance and Johnson, hiked out to Tioga Pass and reported the accident to rangers.

Rangers from Tuolumne Meadows were flown in to the victim's location by the park helicopter. Johnson was hypothermic and Rangers Eric Gabriel and Dave Page began rewarming the patient and stabilizing him for transport. Johnson was to be short hauled to Dana Meadows by the park helicopter but severe down drafts prevented this from occurring. After some difficulty the helicopter was able to set down approximately 100 yards from the victim. The victim was then belayed down in the litter by rescue team members over treacherous terrain to the helicopter. The litter belay took approximately an hour to complete. Johnson was then loaded on the helicopter and flown to Dana Meadows to an awaiting ambulance from Tuolumne Meadows. ALS procedures were initiated and the patient was transferred to June Lake Paramedics for transport to Mammoth Hospital. All rescue team members were flown to Dana Meadows. SAR team members were sent in the following day on foot to retrieve equipment left at the accident site from the night before. Rescue work on the glacier took place with rockfall activity from above.

Johnson sustained an unstable compression fracture to T-8 and L-1, an ankle fracture, and possible facial fractures. Vance was advised to seek medical care as a precaution, due to the nature and distance of the fall. (Source: Dave Page, Ranger, Yosemite National Park)

Analysis
These two had experience as rock climbers—not a lot, but not beginners. They had taken a snow and ice course. This was to be their first snow and ice climb on their own. They were prepared to bivouac, climbing with good sized packs. While it is not known as to what caused the fall, the combination of being new to snow and ice, no protection, and heavy packs resulted in sustaining serious injury. (Source: Dave Page, John Dill, Rangers, Yosemite National Park)

PROTECTION PULLED OUT, FALL ON ROCK, INADEQUATE BELAY, OFF ROUTE
California, Yosemite Valley, El Capitan
On August 6, 1992, Jamie Serrano (25) and Angel Vedo Fernandez (39)—both from Spain, were climbing the Nose route of El Capitan, and were at a location 1200 to 1500 feet above the valley floor, a few pitches below Dolt Tower. Vedo was leading and Serrano was belaying him from a small ledge when Vedo fell and landed on Serrano. Serrano sustained incapacitating injuries.

The two remained on the belay ledge and began yelling for help. An unidentified visitor reported the cries for help to a tour bus operator who radioed the situation to his dispatcher, who in turn telephoned Yosemite Ranger Dispatch with the initial situation information.

Ranger John Roth responded to size-up, confirming that cries for help were coming from the Nose route. An Incident Command System was initiated, with the Yosemite NPS helicopter deployed for a recon flyby. This flyby, utilizing Park Ranger Gus Martinez' Spanish language speaking abilities, revealed that only Serrano was injured, and that a technical evacuation would be required due to back injuries. A rescue plan was formulated that deployed a ground response ascent team comprised of NPS SAR Tech Mike Ray, and Yose SAR site members Tom Borges, Francis Ross, Mike Callahan, and Jim Red. This response team began climbing at 1600, with the assignment to attempt to reach the victims, medically assess, stabilize, and provide helivac support on site.

In the interim, the Lemoore NAS Angel 2 helicopter was requested, which arrived at the El Capitan meadow at 1750. Air operations were staged at the El Capitan Meadow. NPS SAR Tech John Dill then was heli-rappelled, via the Angel 2, to the victim. Next a Lemoore NAS Corpsman heli-rappelled to the ledge, secured the uninjured climber Vedo, and short hauled him and the climbers' equipment off to the El Capitan Meadow. The Angel 2 ship then picked up rescue gear to include medical supplies and a Stokes litter, flew them back to the ledge where they were lowered to John Dill, who was medically assessing the victim.

NPS Ranger John Roth then was flown to the ledge, where he heli-rappelled to Dill and the victim at which time Dill and Roth then immobilized Serrano, packaged him in the Stokes litter and prepared him for the heli-evacuation.

Shortly before darkness, at 2028, Angel 2 hoisted Serrano's litter up to the helicopter and flew him to El Capitan meadow where he was met by the Valley ambulance. Ranger John Roth accompanied him during this hoisting operation. Serrano was immediately driven to the Yosemite Medical Clinic where preliminary medical evaluation indicated that he had sustained a L-1 compression fracture and possibly lacerated liver. He was then transported by ground ambulance to the John C. Fremont Hospital in Mariposa. (Source: James Tucker, Ranger, Yosemite National Park)

Analysis
Serrano and Vedo are very experienced rock climbers and mountaineers, having climbed world-wide for several years, both free and aid, at a high standard.

They made the pendulum from Sickle Ledge (7th pitch) but got off route at that point by following a crack up and right for a pitch to a small ledge about 50 feet right of the Stove Leg Cracks. (A two-bolt anchor at this ledge is part of the Nose rappel route.) Vedo led the next pitch up the crack while Serrano belayed. He was standing on the ledge, belaying with the rope rigged through the large hole of a figure-eight descender in rappel fashion.

After climbing 30 to 40 feet, Vedo leaned back on a Friend he had just placed, to take a photo. Without warning the Friend pulled and Vedo fell. The belay friction may have been inadequate and/or the fall may have caught Serrano off guard, for he allowed several feet of rope to run. (Vedo thought Serrano had been holding the rope with only one hand.) Other protection held and Serrano arrested the fall, but Vedo landed hard on Serrano's chest. (Source: John Dill, SAR Ranger, Yosemite National Park)

FALL ON ROCK
California, Yosemite Valley, Nutcracker
On September 20, 1992, Margaret Cashman was leading the sixth pitch of the Nutcracker route when she took a ten foot leader fall. As a result of the fall she impacted both of her heels causing possible fractures and significant pain. A technical lowering operation with an attending medic was implemented and Cashman was safely brought to the ground and transported to LMH without complication.

Analysis
I don't know exactly what happened here, but we've had several accidents on this pitch, the last on the climb. Just above the start of the pitch is a short, steep corner, then a mantle, then an easy traverse right for a few feet, then a couple of face moves. People have fallen on all of those sections. If not carefully protected, they smack the low-angle slab at the belay. (Source: John Dill, SAR Ranger, Yosemite National Park)

FALL ON ROCK, INADEQUATE PROTECTION
California, Yosemite Valley, Half Dome
On September 17, 1992, a report of an injured climber, Rolf Schempp (25), seven pitches up the Regular Northwest Face route of Half Dome was received by NPS dispatch. A

ranger was inserted at the scene by heli-rappelling from the park contracted helicopter. When the victim was stabilized in a litter, a Navy UH-helicopter from NAS Lemoore attempted to evacuate him. However, the winds were too turbulent to attempt the hoist operation and it was aborted. A short time later the park contract helicopter was able to successfully short haul the victim from Half Dome directly to the Ahwahnee Meadow. The ranger and the victim's climbing partner then rappelled off the route and hiked out.

Analysis

While hiking down the trail from Half Dome, I interviewed Schempp's partner, Jurgen, who told me that they had planned to climb the standard Northwest Face of Half Dome in a day. They were traveling lightly, with minimal food, water and extra clothing. He felt they both were climbing safely and carefully, although he admitted that on the easy sections it was hard to concentrate on properly placing protection. He felt that both he and Rolf would just move quickly with minimal protection on easier sections. The pitch that Rolf fell on, the seventh pitch, is rated at 5.5 in difficulty. At 0910 Rolf fell from the seventh pitch approximately 30 feet before being stopped. Rolf had not placed any protection. Jurgen felt that Rolf used a loose rock as a hold, and when he raised himself on it, the rock detached from the mountain, along with Rolf. Rolf sustained injuries to his head, right hip, and right foot. He never lost consciousness, and moved a short distance from where he landed to the ledge I found him on.

Before I left the stance in the afternoon with Jurgen, I also spoke with John Terpening, a solo climber who was using the same belay stance. He told me that he observed Rolf fall above him, and the belay rope was between him and the wall. In effect, Terpening acted as an intermediate protection point for Rolf. Terpening also told me that this was the second climber he had observed fall past him in the five days he had been on the wall. (Source: Michael LaLone, Ranger, Yosemite National Park)

FALL ON RAPPEL—LOST CONTROL AND DESCENDED TOO RAPIDLY
California, Yosemite Valley, El Capitan

On September 17, 1992, Robert Moore (42) was rappelling a single 7/16 inch, 820 meter rope down the face of El Capitan when he apparently lost control and slid to his death.

Moore was part of a group of about 20 people who had come and fixed ropes on both El Cap and Half Dome. Members of the group had varying goals, from rappelling and climbing both routes to just rappelling El Cap. Moore planned only to rappel El Cap.

Analysis

It appears several factors played a significant role in the accident. These include the specific mechanics of the accident, Moore's apparently casual attitude about safety, and the dynamics of the group of people who were involved with this project.

Moore, and most of the rappellers in his group, passed the top edge by "brute force." When beginning a rappel in this manner, the full weight of the rope must be held off the edge by the rappeller. This can require considerable effort with a heavy rope. On El Cap, the rope weighed 68 kilograms (150 pounds).

At the top edge of the rappel, the rappeller's weight is not supported by the friction of the rappel rack on the rope. The rappeller must adjust the rack to provide little enough friction that it can be pulled along the rope without using the rappeller's weight. Once the rappeller has passed the edge, it is necessary to add more friction to support the rappeller's full weight. If the needed extra friction can't be provided by sliding the bottom bar up toward the rest of the bars, it is necessary to add another bar. It can be difficult to add a bar on a long rappel because the rappeller needs to push the heavy rope to the side while holding on to keep from sliding down the rope.

A haul system can be used to raise the weight of the rope, allowing the rappeller to pass the edge without lifting the rope. Because the weight of the rope is not pulling on the rack, more bars are used when backing over the edge. Once below the edge, a rappeller need only hold a stop long enough to allow the haul system to be released. Once the weight of the rope is back on the rack, the rappeller has more friction than will allow them to move. They can then reduce friction to a level that allows a comfortable descent.

Ted Farmer, a local caver who had rappelled El Capitan with Moore once before, was unable to stop on the rope for the first 250 meters when he did the rappel with Moore's group and brute forced the edge. He had no trouble during his previous rappels, where a haul system was used. He was also unable to stop during our tests where he used gear like Moore's. Starting in this manner could have put Moore into a situation where he was struggling from the start.

Moore passed the top edge with four bars on his rack engaged. At the base, he had four bars engaged. Based on our experiments, he probably would not have been comfortable free hanging with fewer than five bars. According to witnesses, who saw him only once, he was below the lip, Moore rappelled for about 100 meters (328 feet) at a moderate speed, then came to a stop. He may have been able to add a fifth bar just below the lip. It seems more likely that, like Farmer, he was unable to stop or add any bars until he was well below the lip. The exact mechanical means by which Moore lost control are not known. Several mechanisms seem to fit the data.

If Moore had five bars on, he probably removed one when he was stopped. If the spacers on his rack compressed during the upper part of his rappel, that could have increased the friction enough that he decided to continue the rappel with four bars. This would account for his moving so slowly, seemingly pushing the rope through the rack, just before he stopped, as was described by one witness. Moore's grip may then have slipped on the rope with the reduced friction of four bars or he may have just been unable to hold on.

If Moore had four bars engaged, he may have lost his grip while trying to add a fifth bar. He may have been pushing the rope in the wrong direction while attempting to add a fifth bar, allowing a fourth bar to fall to the bottom of the rack and greatly reducing the friction. His grip may have slipped either immediately or while attempting to bring the fourth bar back up. This mechanism, of pushing the rope in the wrong direction when trying to add a bar, has been implicated in some caving accidents in the Tennessee-Alabama-Georgia area.

The following items suggest that Moore had a relaxed attitude about his personal safety: (1) The handout that had been distributed to Moore's group stated that everyone rappelling, whether they planned on climbing or not, would do the rappel with full rope climbing gear. Moore rappelled without any climbing gear. He did not have anything with which to grab the rope. (2) Moore rappelled to the edge on a short tail rope, then switched his rappel rack over to the main line without clipping in a separate safety. (3) When Moore found it difficult to move at the edge with six bars, he dropped the friction immediately to four bars without trying five. (He may have mistakenly gone to three bars before correcting to four.) (4) Moore seems not to have passed the tail of the waist loop on his harness back through the buckle as it should have been. (5) Moore may have been wishing to celebrate his birthday, the day of the rappel, with a very fast descent.

There are some observations regarding the group that may also have had some bearing on the situation. Moore was not involved at all in fixing the ropes. The ropes had been in place for nearly a week when Moore and Doherty arrived in the park. There may have been a sense of competitiveness among various members of the group, particularly since they seem to have been concerned with record setting. Because he didn't know Moore better, one of the people at the top, Coney, did not feel comfortable telling Moore that he was being unsafe, or that he should have rope climbing gear with him. The group was not a team but rather a collection of individuals. In such a group, people are not as careful to "watch out" for others in the party, and do not feel responsible for doing so.

Whatever the mechanism of the failure or the influence of his attitude or that of the group, we know Moore was making adjustments to his belay chain without being backed up by another system. A spelean shunt could have been on the rope as a safety during his entire rappel. If he had a Jumar or similar ascender, which can be placed on the rope with one hand, he could have set that as a back up when he stopped to make adjustments. (Source: Michael D. Ray, SAR Ranger, Yosemite National Park)

(Editor's Note: Many non-climbers attempt a variety of feats in the mountain environment. The National Park Service—and custodians of climbing areas in general—have little choice but to categorize any incidents that result from these feats as mountain/climbing accidents. Scramblers, "rappellers," individuals who decide to try climbing—on an impulse, and so forth, continue to draw the attention of the media when they get in trouble and require rescue.)

FALLING ROCK
California, Yosemite National Park, Mount Dana
On September 27, 1992, John Hart (44) was belaying David Sanger (43) one pitch above the bergschrund on the left hand side of the Couloir on the Dana Glacier. Hart was about 20 to 30 feet away from the rock wall and anchored. He was unable to dodge a football sized rock that was coming down the Couloir. The rock struck his right patella. The force also resulted in fractures to the shaft and medial condoyle of the femur and to the top of the tibia.

Hart continued to belay his partner up to his position. A rescue operation ensued, involving other climbers, two rangers, a helicopter, and an ambulance. (Source: K. L. O'Connor-Henry, Ranger, Yosemite National Park)

Analysis
While there was no comment provided regarding (a) the position of the climber in the couloir or (b) whether this is an area of known spontaneous rockfall, it is an illustrative accident for consideration of the common factors, either of which can result in injury. (Source: Jed Williamson)

PROTECTION PULLED OUT, FALL ON ROCK
California, Yosemite Valley, El Capitan
On October 12, 1992, at 0730, Doug Chabot (28) was leading the 26th pitch of the Nose Route, El Capitan. He was aiding up a crack 40 feet out from the belay ledge (Camp

Five). While standing on a TCU (#0 or #1), it popped from the crack. He also pulled the stopper below the TCU. He fell about 20 feet, landing on a ledge in a sitting position. The impact caused severe pain in his lower thoracic/upper lumbar spine. He did not lose consciousness, and was able to lower himself the further 20 feet to Camp V. The other two members of his party waited for about two hours before they determined that Chabot was unable to ascend or descend due to the severe pain in his back. His companions, Todd McDougal and Steve House, decided to continue up the route and once on top, descend and obtain help. Chabot spent the remainder of the day on the Camp V ledge system. McDougal and House were able to report the accident at 2040. They reported that Chabot's condition was extremely stable, his pulse and respirations were in normal limits, and he would be able to spend the night without seriously compromising his injuries.

An I.C. overhead team was established and plans made for the following day. Due to extremely good weather conditions and the availability of the Park Contract Helicopter (H-51), it was decided to conduct all initial operations via air. This allowed most personnel involved a good night's sleep without the requirement of hiking a ground team in from Tamarack Flat Campground.

Operations began at 0700 on October 13. Rangers were lowered to Chabot. They stabilized him, then raised him 900 vertical feet to the top, where he was then flown to the valley and transported to Yosemite Medical Clinic. He had sustained a compression fracture of his L-1 vertebrae, and various fractured bones in his left hand.

Analysis
I interviewed Stephen House regarding the skill levels of all three climbers. He advised me that all three members of the party had between four and eleven years of climbing experience individually. All three are guides with the American Alpine Institute, and climbing/guiding concession at Cascades. All had experience with wall climbing before, although this was Chabot's first Grade VI climb. When asked why they chose to climb to the top to obtain help rather than yelling for help, House advised me the thought never occurred to them. He was unaware that their cries would travel to the ground clearly enough to be heard. As most of their experience was in a remote wilderness environment, they were not used to the concept of merely shouting for help. (Source: Michael LaLone, Ranger, Yosemite National Park)

PROTECTION PULLED OUT, FALL ON ROCK, INADEQUATE SELF-BELAY (SLACK IN ROPE)
California, Yosemite Valley, El Capitan
On Tuesday, October 13, 1992, Mark Ousley (32) began a roped solo ascent of the Shield (VI 5.9 A3). That day he climbed another party's fixed lines to Heart Ledge and then climbed the pitch to Mammoth Terrace, where he spent the night. He was belaying himself with the Solo Aid device (made by Rock Exotica). This device, intended primarily for aid climbing, requires that the rope be manually pulled through it.

Wednesday morning he started up the eleventh pitch of the Shield, a mostly low-angle, easy free pitch with a steeper 5.9 section near its top. Just below the 5.9 section Ousely gave himself ten to 15 feet of slack, so that he would not have to readjust the rope until he was past the hard moves. He also placed two secure Friends and distributed the load between them with a sling. He moved up a few feet and placed a #0.5 Lowe Tri-Cam in a piton pocket and yanked on it a couple of times, to set it. The piece looked marginal but he felt it would catch and hold if it shifted.

Although he had intended to continue free-climbing, the next moves looked harder than he wanted to do, so he decided to pull himself up on the Tri-Cam and then go free again. He looked down and saw that the two Friends were only about four feet below him; despite the low angle wall below, he felt his protection was adequate, so he put his weight on the Tri-Cam. As he did so, it pulled out. The fall should have been a short one, but he had neglected to reduce the slack in his rope before making the aid move; he fell about 25 feet, striking a small ledge with his left foot just before he stopped.

He knew immediately that his foot was injured. He removed his shoe and saw that the foot was severely deformed and bleeding— almost certainly he had an open fracture or dislocation. He could lie down where he was, so he did so and raised his leg to slow the bleeding.

Two climbers on the Salathe route witnessed the fall. They rappelled two pitches to Heart Ledge and climbed to Ousley. The three of them managed to splint his leg with an ace bandage and a piton hammer and lower him to Mammoth Terrace (about 35 feet). Meanwhile the NPS was notified by climbers at the base of the wall. Ranger Kelly McCloskey rappelled to Mammoth Terrace from the park helicopter, dressed and splinted Ousley's leg, and short hauled him to the Valley floor under the helicopter. At the medical clinic he was found to have suffered a severe, open, subtalar dislocation with some probable small fractures. Repairing it will require at least three operations, but he is expected to regain almost all function.

Analysis

At the time of his accident, Ousley had nine or ten years of climbing experience, led 5.10 A3 or better, and had previously climbed six Grade VI routes on El Capitan, including a solo ascent of Tangerine Trip. Ousley feels that he was not being too hasty with his climbing but rather too confident (although the distinction may be a narrow one). He had not forgotten the slack in his rope when he checked his protection, but neglected to readjust it before weighting the marginal piece. He was experienced with the Solo Aid, having used it on two other Grade VIs and having had previous falls successfully arrested by it.

During his recovery Mike Ousley sent me additional information regarding his accident. I have transcribed it, with minor editing, below:

It is important to understand that, regardless of the system used, a much greater distinction exists between 'free' and 'aid' when roped-solo climbing than with the conventional two-person system. Because of the relatively slow and predictable movement of climbing on aid, belaying can be more easily managed by the soloing leader, especially considering the hands-free status that can be obtained at nearly every protection point along the pitch. Conversely, during free climbing, the leader moves much more quickly, one or both hands may be occupied through sections of the pitch, and slack may need to be taken in and let out. Simply put, it is much easier to solo climb at one's limit on aid than free.

When big-wall climbing, the leader may switch between aid and free in a single pitch, or may employ the so-called 'French-free' technique—using free-climbing gear for resting in or ascending difficult sections without the usual ensemble of aid-specific gear. So there exists a point where the big-wall leader is neither exclusively free climbing or aid climbing, but going French-free because the terrain may be judged too difficult to free climb or can be more expediently ascended using this technique.

As a soloist I believe I could have reduced or eliminated my injury in one of the following ways: (1) By not employing French-free technique and by treating the pitch, or at least the difficult section, as A1. (This is not always possible, depending on available protection.) (2) By equipping myself more for a free pitch, and not (or less) specifically for aid climbing. For example, wearing free-climbing footwear, carrying a chalk bag, choosing the most modern and lightweight equipment to protect the next pitch, considering all other ways to lighten the leader's load such as leaving hammer and pitons in haulbag, using nine or ten mm haul line, etc. (3) By selecting an aid-climbing route that contains the least amount of free climbing (and the easiest). (Source: Kerry Maxwell, Ranger, Yosemite National Park)

AVALANCHE, EUPHORIA FROM GOOD WEATHER AND PERFECT BACKCOUNTRY SKIING, NOT HEEDING INDICATIONS OF INSTABILITY, PARTY SEPARATED
Colorado, San Juan Mountains

Four of us from New England were skiing powder gullies and open trees below peak 12,311 in the Sneffels Range in the San Juan Mountains of southwest Colorado. We had spent two nights in nearby Last Dollar hut where we met two skiers from Utah. February 25 began clear and cold as all six of us skinned up the ridge. The day warmed into perfect skiing weather by mid morning. With a blue sky and 30 to 40 cm of well-settled powder, conditions could not be better. We had completed two runs each by noon, in the relative safety of so-called Gully 1A. This was recommended by local skiers. Its pitch did not exceed 15 degrees.

On the first run, we skied one at a time and stayed near the trees. We were concerned about avalanches. A shovel shear test the day before indicated a weak layer at 50 cm. The avalanche forecast was MODERATE (three days earlier). However, our concern for avalanches lessened as the day progressed. In the afternoon the group had divided into pairs. Rob and I were standing in a safe location at the top of Gully No. 1A when we glimpsed Bob and Steve entering Gully No. 2 in search of new powder. We paused to discuss possible hazards.

We were staring at the headwall to the northeast just above Gully No. 2 when it fractured sequentially in three places, zippering across the entire wall. We yelled, "AVALANCHE!" but no one heard. We were shocked as we knew all four people below were exposed to the danger. We heard no calls from below. Time 1350. We discussed alternative search routes and decided to descend 1A and intersect the slide lower down. This was the slowest descent I have ever made... time seemed to stand still. Part way down we heard Sally calling and knew someone was safe.

We were all properly equipped with transceivers, shovels, and probe poles. All were experienced backcountry skiers. The proper steps for self-rescue raced through my mind as we descended. By the time we were within yelling distance, we learned only Steve Gordon (39) was missing. Bob had been able to ski out of the avalanche path. Sally and Dave had just completed their run and found themselves just on the edge of the run out zone.

By the time we reached the bottom, Bob had located Steve's "beep" and the group was digging. Steve was buried for less than 20 minutes under less than a meter of debris. However, excavating him was very difficult as his body and equipment were entangled with a tree. Attempts to resuscitate the victim with CPR were unsuccessful. The body was removed the next day by helicopter under directions of the San Miguel Sheriff's Department. Cause of death: asphyxiation and massive head trauma.

The side path was estimated to 500 meters long and 250 meters vertical. The fracture zone was 120 meters wide by one m at its initiation point (an unseen pillow on the steeper west face of the bowl). However, most of the fracture wall was merely 20 to 30 cm high. The release was said to be "skier triggered from below."

Analysis

(1) Our test pit was dug on an aspect equivalent to what we skied, not that of the slope across the other side of the bowl. (2) We were skiing below a slope exceeding 30. (3) The euphoria of beautiful weather, scenery, and turns in perfect powder overshadowed caution after several runs. (4) Local advice and the avalanche forecast were weighted too heavily in the light of our field observation. (5) The prevailing wind had been northwest for several days, leaving the northwest facing bowl relatively safe. Apparently, a northeast eddy had windloaded a small, unnoticed area of slab on the far wall. (6) The victim was skiing with a heavy pack loaded with camera equipment. Possibly this reduced his mobility. (7) The skiers had too much separation to hear warning calls. (8) On our upclimb along the edge of the woods, "whoomp" sounds gave a strong indication of instability. (Source: Jed Eliades—53)

(Editor's Note: A fund in memory of Steve Gordon has been established by his friends. Contributions received are designated for the AAC Safety Committee.)

STRANDED, POOR COMMUNICATIONS, INEXPERIENCE, WEATHER
Colorado, Rocky Mountain National Park, Twin Owls
On June 9, 1992, at 1000, Brandon Latham (20) and Tom Anderson (19) began an ascent of Twin Owls via the East Ridge I (5.8). At 1200 Anderson was at the top of the second or final pitch, and he began to belay Latham. At this point, an intense thunderstorm had moved into the area, bringing with it loud thunder, bursts of lightning, and heavy rain. Anderson and Latham were unable to communicate with each other. Latham assumed Anderson would be rappelling down, so he untied himself from the rope. Anderson assumed Latham was climbing, and pulled in all of the slack rope until he found the untied rope end, minus Latham. Still unable to communicate with Latham, Anderson climbed over the top of Twin Owls and descended the "Bowells" to get help. Rangers Rick Guerrieri and Rik Henrikson responded by rappelling to Latham's location from the top. Latham was assessed for possible hypothermia and then lowered to the ground.

Analysis
Poor communications due to noisy environmental conditions is the cause of this incident, which could have evolved into something even worse. It is imperative that climbing partners agree on a set of silent signals, such as a series or rope tugs, before they ever start a pitch. In any case, the partner should never untie himself from the rope when communications are unclear, especially in the middle of a multiple-pitch climb. (Source: Jim Detterline, Longs Peak Supervisory Climbing Ranger, Rocky Mountain National Park)

AVALANCHE, LOSS OF CONTROL—GLISSADING, POOR ROUTE FINDING
Colorado, San Juan Mountains, Lookout Peak
I was mountain climbing with my husband, Edward W. Enlow, Jr. (38), when he had a fatal mountaineering accident on June 13, 1992. The following is a description of the accident.

We had decided to climb Lookout Peak, a 13,661 foot mountain in the San Juan mountain range near Ophir Pass in Colorado. We had read descriptions of the climb in various books, but we did not have a topographical map of the mountain. Soon after we started to climb, we were off trail and hiking up steep, snowy slopes toward a false summit. After we reached the false summit, we looked for a route to the true summit. That route led us over an exposed ridge with loose snow and then up a steep rock couloir on the north side of the mountain. We reached the summit at 1430, much later than we had anticipated when we started the climb. Since the skies were clear and sunny, Ed wasn't concerned about the late ascent.

When we started the descent at 1445, the snow was quite soft. We decided to try to descend by the "standard" route, which was most likely covered in snow, but we could not find an easy way down. After descending 100 feet of steep rock on the south side of the mountain, Ed decided to attempt a seated glissade down a steep snow chute. He had assumed that the chute would be snow covered all the way down to gentler terrain about 500 feet below. However, when he started his glissade, a small avalanche followed him into the chute. I yelled out to him to get out of the chute since he didn't see the avalanche behind him. He tried to self-arrest twice, without success, since he was caught in the swiftly moving snow. He then disappeared out of my sight.

I started to carefully descend down the same chute and saw exposed rocks below due to the avalanche having cleared away the loose snow. I also saw a cliff below me instead of a gradual slope. I had to find a different way down. Using extreme caution (while starting to go into shock at the unknown condition of my husband), I traversed across a couple of steep snow chutes, walked under a huge, cracked cornice, and descended a steep rock and snow gully. I saw his body below with his daypack about 20 feet away from his body. I reached his body about 30 minutes later. His arm was broken but there were no open wounds or external bleeding. There was no pulse or bleeding. The autopsy revealed that internal bleeding was the cause of death and that he had experienced a free fall which killed him instantly upon impact.

Analysis

Knowledge of dangerous snow conditions would help. Make sure the whole runout of a snow chute is visible before starting a glissade.

Climbers must never take a casual attitude toward mountains.... We always have to respect the dangers of mountaineering, even after having climbed successfully for many years. (Source: Regina Pasquale)

LIGHTNING, LATE START, INEXPERIENCE
Colorado, Rocky Mountain National Park, Hallett Peak

On June 28, 1992, at 2100, Glenn R. McDonald (31) was struck and killed by lightning near the summit of Hallett Peak after ascending Hallett Chimney II (5.6). McDonald and his partner Wayne Smart were attempting to summit when the incident occurred. Smart attempted CPR, but there was no response from McDonald.

Analysis

Smart had intermediate climbing skills, but McDonald was a beginner. They did not know each other prior to the climb. They had met through a "climbing partner wanted" ad on the bulletin board of a Boulder mountaineering shop. They had initially planned to do the Culp-Bossier Route III (5.8), but could not locate the start, so did Hallett Chimney instead. They finished the technical portion of the route by about 2000. Although they noticed a prominent electrical storm in progress on nearby Longs Peak, they thought it would be safe to continue to Hallett Peak's summit.

McDonald and Smart had a very late start. They were contacted by Ranger Vicki Steele at 0930, at Dream Lake, less than halfway to the start of their destination. Steele cautioned them about the hazards of starting late. They said they were aware of these. Their inexperience at alpine route-finding also slowed them down. It is recommended that climbers start their routes at first light so they are headed down before the afternoon thunderstorms arrive. Finally, alpine climbs are no place for "blind dates." It's better to meet on an easy rock climb to test each other's skills. (Source: Jim Detterline, Longs Peak Supervisory Climbing Ranger, Rocky Mountain National Park)

FALL ON ROCK, CLIMBING ALONE AND UNROPED, EXCEEDING ABILITIES
Colorado, Rocky Mountain National Park, Mount Meeker

On July 29, 1992, Mrs. Melinda Boyer reported that her husband Gary Boyer (35) was overdue from a July 28 solo attempt of Mount Meeker. The ensuing search effort in stormy weather by park rangers and a contract helicopter culminated at 1455 with the discovery by rangers Dave Herrick and Andy Brown of the body of Gary Boyer. He was found about 400 feet up technical terrain in the gully on the right side of the East Arete on Mount Meeker. Recovery efforts included a technical litter lowering, several hundred feet of scree evacuation, and a 0.25 mile litter carry to a backcountry helispot, where the victim was picked up by helicopter after inclement weather had subsided.

Analysis

An investigation into the accident revealed that Boyer had attempted the 5.7 rock face on Meeker solo and unroped. A hiker had seen a person believed to be Boyer near the summit ridge, unroped solo, and apparently having some difficulty ascending a section of steep rock at 1200 on July 28. Based on the extent of Boyer's injuries and the position of the solo climber as witnessed, it is believed that Boyer died as the result of a slip on rock resulting in a 1000 foot fall. Boyer had been climbing once or twice per year for four years. (Source: Jim Detterline, Longs Peak Supervisory Climbing Ranger, Rocky Mountain National Park)

FALL ON SNOW, INADEQUATE BELAY—CLIMBING UNROPED
Colorado, Rocky Mountain National Park, Longs Peak

On August 9, 1992, at 0900, Andy Griffiths (36) was attempting to climb Lamb's Slide on the East face of Longs Peak. He slipped and slid 300 feet, sustaining injuries to his left elbow, hip, and ankle. Charlie McVey reached and assessed Griffiths, and then used his portable ham radio to contact Dan St. John in Fort Collins, Colorado. St. John then reported the incident to Rocky Mountain National Park Rangers, and continued to provide the rescue team with updates from the scene until reached by the rescue team and an air ambulance helicopter.

Analysis

Mr. Griffiths' accident is one that has been repeated continuously through the years on Lamb's Slide. Some of these slides have resulted in fatalities. Once the icy conditions of mid-summer appear on Lamb's Slide, it is almost impossible to self-arrest. To prevent a really long fall, it is not very time consumptive to set up a tandem climbing situation by roping up and moving together while attached to placements generally on the right rock wall.

The unique aspect of this accident is the use of portable communications by the citizen in order to expedite the rescue effort. Park Rescue has been contacted via ham radio and cellular telephone an increasing number of times in recent years. Several of these contacts during cases of life-threatening injuries, such as two hikers struck by lightning at the Boulder Field on Longs Peak, resulted in quick medical responses that saved lives. (Source: Jim Detterline, Longs Peak Supervisory Climbing Ranger, Rocky Mountain National Park)

FALL ON ROCK, CLIMBING UNROPED, EXCEEDING ABILITIES
Colorado, Rocky Mountain National Park, Little Matterhorn

On August 16, 1992, at 1000, Jon M. Hofstra (23) fell about 1000 feet while descending unroped from the summit of the Little Matterhorn down the fourth class and lower fifth class northeast chimneys route. Partners Todd Feenstra and Andrew Tenbrink were able to continue their descent, reaching Hofstra in an hour. It was determined that Hofstra was dead, and Rocky Mountain National Park Rangers were contacted to conduct a helicopter recovery of the body.

Analysis

Hofstra and his partners were climbing an easy technical route without rope and proper belay techniques. The Hofstra group was an enthusiastic but inexperienced team on a day off from a University field camp. (Source: Jim Detterline, Longs Peak Supervisory Climbing Ranger, Rocky Mountain National Park)

FALL ON ROCK, PLACED INADEQUATE PROTECTION, ICY ROCK
Colorado, Rocky Mountain National Park, Longs Peak

On September 19, 1992, at 0830, Lathe Strang (30) fractured his left ankle as he slipped on icy rock while leading the first pitch of Prevertical Sanctuary IV (5.10) on the Diamond face of Longs Peak. Strang was 30 feet above the belay and eight feet above his last piece of protection, a #3.5 Friend. He suffered a 20 foot fall and struck his left foot against rock upon impact from the fall. Climbers George Lowe and Alex Lowe responded to the calls of Erik Hendrix, Strang's partner, and lowered the injured climber down the lower East Face 800 feet. They continued to assist Strang across Mills Glacier and through the tundra to meet with the Rocky Mountain National Park Rescue Unit at Chasm Meadows.

George Lowe and Alex Lowe are to be commended for their efficient, professional rescue of the Strang-Hendrix party. They had completed the East Face lowering before the park service even got the word that there had been an accident.

Analysis

Strang was aware of icy conditions on the Diamond when he attempted his lead. He was hoping that conditions higher on the route would be drier. He had not even reached the 5.9 crux before he slipped on the icy rock. If unable to handle the eccentricities of free climbing on icy rock, one should either aid the pitch, or at least place protection more frequently. Of course, if either of these alternatives compromises the ability of a party to safely and efficiently finish a route, retreat should be executed. (Source: Jim Detterline, Longs Peak Supervisory Climbing Ranger, Rocky Mountain National Park)

STRANDED, INADEQUATE EQUIPMENT, EXCEEDING ABILITIES
Colorado, Rocky Mountain National Park, Lumpy Ridge

On September 2, 1992, at 1615, Nan Derkiss (30) and John Quackenbush became stranded when they got their rope stuck on the second pitch of Pear Buttress II (5.8+) on the Book on Lumpy Ridge. Ranger Scott Metcalfe and Colorado Mountain School guide Lawrence Stuempke ascended to free the Derkiss/Quackenbush rope, and then led the couple on the remainder of the four pitch route using Metcalf's ropes.

Analysis
The second pitch of Pear Buttress begins with a short traverse before a move upward into a long crack system. It is advisable to do the short traverse as a single pitch, and then do the crack system as another pitch. Many parties get hung up at this particular spot. However, any party on a multiple pitch route should be competent at self-rescue. Carrying a set of prusik loops would allow one to anchor the rope and ascend or descend to the source of trouble. (Source: Jim Detterline, Longs Peak Supervisory Climbing Ranger, Rocky Mountain National Park)

AVALANCHE, WEATHER
Colorado, Rocky Mountain National Park, Flattop Mountain

On November 1, 1992, Brad Farnan (30), Todd Martin (24) and two female climbers were practicing snow climbing techniques on the Central Couloir, Northwest Face of Flattop Mountain. The women decided to turn around at the junction with the West Couloir. While descending, they were within the protection of a rock island when they felt what was described as a "strange wind" coming down the Central Couloir, along with one of Martin's gloves. Visibility had been poor all day, and they were unable to establish voice contact. Park Rangers were contacted, and a massive search effort took place in what had turned into the first really major storm of the season, with some rescuers in snow up to their shoulders despite snowshoes. On November 3, the packs of the missing climbers were observed about 400 feet from the top of the climb. As of January 1, 1993, the climbers have not yet been located and are believed dead from avalanche.

Analysis
Farnan was an experienced and respected mountain guide with Colorado Mountain School. This was a trip among friends, and not a CMS class. He had been climbing and guiding in these gullies of Flattop all during the Autumn season without incident. On the day of his disappearance, conditions in the gully were stable and excellent climbing. (He had also been there the day before.) The storm had just begun to blow in when Farnan started climbing, and had not dropped much precipitation at that point. It is believed that the cornice overhanging the route broke while the climbers were taking a break on a ledge.

It was unusual for the cornice to have persisted this late in the season. On this mountain face, the cornices generally form at the beginning of winter, and drop off in late spring to early summer. Although Farnan correctly judged conditions on the route itself, there was no way of knowing that the cornice had been sufficiently weakened to unload. Climbing beneath this sort of feature is a calculated risk of mountaineering, and the cornice failed despite passing all the usual tests such as sufficient cold weather, no visible cracks or weaknesses, and no previous unloading. (Source: Jim Detterline, Longs Peak Supervisory Climbing Ranger, Rocky Mountain National Park)

(Editor's Note: In 1992, according to Rocky Mountain National Park Chief Ranger Joseph Evans, there were 314 SAR callouts, 34 of which involved technical climbers. But 25 of these were "overdue" parties, and only four of them were significant in terms of manpower and expenditures of money. In three of these cases, three climbers were fatalities. Seven callouts involved technical climbers in trouble—some of whom were experienced, some of whom were beginners. The point to be made is that climbers—as opposed to hikers and scramblers—accounted for only a small percentage of the SAR activity overall. However, as we often mention, media and various agencies tend to count all SAR missions in Rocky Mountain National Park, and other parks with a mountain orientation, as "mountaineering" or "mountain related" accidents, lending false credence to the notion that the sport has a high accident rate and is very dangerous.)

INADEQUATE ANCHOR, FALL ON ROCK, FALLING ROCK, FATIGUE, EXCEEDING ABILITIES
Idaho, City of Rocks
On March 25, 1992, Dan Maynes (24) and I (23) were climbing at City of Rocks National Reserve in Southern Idaho. We had both just graduated in Mechanical Engineering. Dan, who had been climbing for two years, had gotten me interested in climbing two months earlier. Due to a mild winter, we had been able to spend 15 to 20 hours per week climbing for the past four weeks in Logan Canyon, just minutes from campus.

This was our second day at City of Rocks. We did not have a guide book for the area, but had been able to find a number of routes we were both able to climb. I did not know the difficulty of the routes I led, but knew that they were more difficult than any I had attempted before. (They had been 5.10d and 5.11a.) I felt great and knew this was the best climbing I had ever done.

Approximately 1730 we headed back to camp to avoid hiking in the dark. We were, however, looking for one last easy climb to finish on. The bolts on a route called "City Girls" located on Flaming Rock caught our eyes. I led the route. About half way up I stopped and exclaimed to Dan that this was a little tougher than I had expected. (It was a 5.10d.) Wanting to finish the day on a high note, I pressed on and finished the route without incident. However, as I reached the chains at the top, I ran into a problem. I did not have a good hold and my tiring forearms told me that I would most likely peel if I freed a hand to attach my last quick draw. I made an impulsive decision to continue on two more feet to reach a wide, 15 foot deep horizontal ledge. There I was able to rest in safety. However, now I could not safely reach down to the chains to rappel back down.

I found 15 feet behind me two nylon climbing slings tied where two rock surfaces were "pinched" together. The rock "pinch" was formed by at least one large table size boulder wedged against the surface of the main crag. I inspected the slings and found both to be tied securely. One was faded and ragged, but the other appeared nearly new.

Using a five foot loop of nylon webbing I had with me and two carabiners, I anchored the back of my harness to the slings. I pulled at the anchor while watching the "pinch" for any movement. It seemed very solid. I then sat down on the edge and belayed Dan up to the top of the climb. Dan untied from the rope as I unhooked myself from the slings. We could stand ten feet from the edge of the ledge so we felt secure even though we were not roped in. I threaded the rope through the sling and gave it a tug that I felt would represent the force it would see during rappelling. Nothing budged. Dan inspected the slings and even tried to move the table size boulder. He gave the anchor his nod of approval. Before he could thread the rope through his rappel device, I stopped him. Sitting on the rock to belay him up the route, I had gotten cold and asked if I could go first. He obliged and I threaded the rope through my figure 8 and approached the edge.

I had never rappelled with a single rappel anchor of this nature before. I had, however, descended using live trees as single anchors. In my mind this set up was equally as stout. This may have been influenced by the fact that I was so cold. I eased myself over the edge to begin the descent. This is all I remember.

According to Dan, just as I disappeared over the lip and out of his sight, he heard a sharp crack behind him and a frightful yelp from below. He saw the climbing rope and large pieces of rock falling over the lip in my direction. Some of the rock hit Dan as it rolled toward the edge. The table size boulder had pivoted and its end that created the pinch had broken off allowing the sling to pull through. I fell helplessly 60 feet to the ground.

Dan yelled frantically to me but there was only deadly silence. He quickly gathered his gear and began searching for a place to down climb. He reached me approximately 15 minutes later. I was lying in a creek at the base of the climb semiconscious and disoriented. The top of the climb was inverted, allowing me to fall feet first touching nothing until I met the ground. The rock that had fallen appeared to have had enough momentum to land away from the base of the route and had not hit me. Dan checked my vitals then left to get help. He quickly found three other climbers nearby. He sent one to the ranger station while the others accompanied him back with sleeping bags to cover me in the near freezing water. The City of Rocks Quick Response Unit, a Burly, Idaho, ambulance and a Life Flight helicopter were summoned. About 2130 I arrived by Life Flight at Bannock Medical Center in Pocatello, Idaho. I do remember the helicopter ride. I remember being in a tremendous amount of pain and not knowing why or what was going on. I was assessed with multiple lacerations, internal injuries and a pelvis broken in two places, allowing my right leg and hip joint to be impacted 3 1/2 inches into my body cavity.

The next afternoon I was flown to the University of Utah Medical Center in Salt Lake City. I remained there for 16 days, returning six weeks later to have two large fixator pins that extended from my hips removed. I was on crutches for five months returning once in June for surgery to correct fractures in my right foot not previously detected. By mid September I was walking slowly without the aid of crutches.

Analysis
I believe that the "pinch" had been a popular rappel anchor and had been used by many climbers, probably even the person who bolted the route nearly 12 years earlier. The fact that there was still a considerable amount of snow in the area means that I could have been the first to use the "pinch" this season. This leads me to believe that the shifting could have been caused by cracks formed during the freeze/thaw cycle.

There are two things that should be gained in reading this account. First, a word of caution: be mindful of the power of erosion and the freeze/thaw cycle in early spring. Second, use a double rappel anchor. ALWAYS! (Source: Darin Ewer)

INADEQUATE BELAY, FALL ON ROCK, LIGHTNING, FEAR
Idaho, City of Rocks, Elephant Rock

On June 20, 1992, Lew Peterson (34) and Mark Parent (35) were climbing "Just Say No" (5.9) when the following accident happened. Peterson was belaying Parent, who had finished leading the climb. Peterson was lowering him using a figure 8 belay device. The 165 foot rope which Peterson was feeding out through his belay device was stored in a rope bag located just behind Peterson. Because the rope was being fed out from the bag, Peterson could not see how much rope was remaining. As Parent was leaning back, being lowered, the last of the rope fed out from the rope bag and ran through Peterson's belay device before he could react. Parent had reached the third bolt (approximately 35 feet above the ground) when the rope became free of Peterson's belay device and Parent fell the remaining distance to the ground. He reportedly landed on his feet and rolled partially down the slope below the climb. Peterson dashed to keep him from rolling and protected his head from hitting the rock. He fractured his pelvis, but has fully recovered.

Analysis

"Just Say No" is approximately 120 feet long and requires two ropes, tied together, to lower or rappel off. The other descent option is to walk off of an easy slope on the back side of Elephant Rock.

Mike Parent was reportedly a very experienced climber while Peterson had only two years of experience. Peterson said that Parent was so comfortable with his rope management skills that he often went too fast for Peterson to be fully prepared or understand the actions before they happened. Peterson also said that he had had several other close calls while climbing with Parent and described Parent as being almost too casual in his climbing. Peterson said that he was initially under the impression that they would walk off after climbing and that when they began the lowering, it did not seem right to him.

Parent added in his own report that both the belayer and climber should be tied in regardless of the length of the rope, and that the belayer needs to be aware of when the mid-point of the rope has passed him. He said further that the plan had been for Parent to belay Peterson from the top anchor and then both would walk off. But as Parent is really afraid of lightning, he decided to be lowered off than to be highly exposed, even for just five minutes. (Sources: Maura Longden, Ranger, City of Rocks National Reserve, and Mark Parent)

INADEQUATE BELAY, INATTENTION, FALL ON ROCK
Idaho, City of Rocks, Rabbit Rock

On Friday, August 7, 1992, at 1300, Andrew (33) and Glenda Lainias (34) were climbing a route called "Sudden Pleasure." Andrew Lainias had reached the top of the climb and was being lowered on the rope by Glenda Lainias. Glenda was controlling his descent by using a Stitchplate belay/friction device. According to one witness, Sherry Grigsby, Glenda Lainias and Grigsby had discussed the fact that using a single rope length to lower Andrew would not adequately allow him to reach the ground. They both believed that one rope length would reach the top of a pillar at the base of the route and that Andrew would be able to safely down climb from there to the ground. While Glenda was lowering Andrew, she was reportedly talking with some of the other people at the base of the climb when she reached the end of the rope and it passed through her belay device before she could react. Andrew had not yet reached the top of the pillar and, when the rope went slack, he fell on to the pillar and then off of it and on to the ground. The total distance of the fall was approximately 30 feet. He suffered only lacerations and contusions.

Analysis
Andrew and Glenda Lainias were reportedly very experienced, competent, safe climbers with 8+ years of rock climbing experience, and many previous years of mountaineering experience. The difficulty of the route, "Sudden Pleasure," and the lowering system which they used for descent were consistent with their past experiences on sport climbs.

Though the route is often descended using one rope and then a down climb to the ground, it is often accomplished by a rappel. (The climbers had reportedly seen someone rappel to within a few feet of the ground from the top of the route just before their climb.) Using the lowering system which the Lainias's chose requires the belayer to move up the rock a few feet to allow the person descending to reach the top of the pillar. With the position of the climber and belayer, the rope was not long enough to accomplish the descent and, without the attention of the belayer on the ground or a knot in the end of the rope to prevent it from passing through the belay device, the rope became free of the belayer. (Source: Maura Longden, Ranger, City of Rocks National Reserve)

(Editor's Note: On August 23, 1992, another climber was being lowered on the same route when the same thing happened. He fell 50 feet, but was uninjured.)

FALL ON ROCK, CAUGHT FOOT ON EDGE, EXCEEDING ABILITIES
Idaho, City of Rocks
On August 29, 1992, Tim Mooney (24) decided to "Pink Point" a route which his partner, Paul Hodges (24), had already led. At the last bolt clip in, which he failed to make, he slipped and fell. Before he could push away from the rock, he caught an edge of rock with his foot, resulting in a fractured ankle. His partner lowered him, carried him out, and drove him to Salt Lake City for treatment.

Analysis
Hodges had recommended to Mooney that he did not feel it was a good day for him to try this route. He stated that the only two ways to have prevented injury would have been not to have led the route or to have fallen in a more controlled way. (Source: Tim Mooney and Paul Hodges)

(Editor's Note: Another sketchy Case Incident Report from the same day indicates that one of the above climbers, Paul Hodges, was belaying a woman on a top rope on "Rye Crisp" when she fell two or three feet and "somehow broke her leg." That's all we know!)

FALL ON ROCK, CLIMBING ALONE AND UNROPED, EXCEEDING ABILITIES
Missouri, Kansas City, Cliff Drive
Cliff Drive is a limestone crag near downtown Kansas City, Missouri. There are six to 12 routes of varying difficulty. I was climbing with friends on October 4, 1992. Two climbers

that we didn't know showed up and one, Russ Engle (19), started climbing the route known as "The Book" (5.9). He was solo climbing and was well within view from the route we were top roping. As he got near the top of the climb, he was obviously having difficulty. He was only a few moves—about eight feet— from the top of the climb when he fell approximately 45 feet, landing on his feet and tumbling over backward after impact. He rolled five to eight feet down a scree type slope where he came to rest. Immediately Bill Leo took control of the situation. Bill is a certified EMT. Chris called for an ambulance on his car phone and Melissa stabilized Russ's head. Engle was in a great deal of pain. An ambulance and emergency help arrived within 15 minutes. He was transported to North Kansas City Hospital where he was listed in critical condition. This was upgraded to serious by 2000 that evening. He sustained two severely broken ankles. (Source: Robert Scheier)

FALLING ROCK, ROCK DISLODGED BY PARTNERS
Montana, Beartooth Mountains
On September 2, 1992, Kimberly Paulson (22) was with seven other members of a Minneapolis, MN, YMCA group when she was struck by a falling rock that had been dislodged by the person in front of her. The rock weighed an estimated one ton. She died from her injuries later that evening, before rescuers arrived. (Source: Star Tribune article, September 4, 1992)

(Editor's Note: This will be reported as a "mountain related" accident to the National Safety Council and other agencies. We call it a hiking accident and do not include it in our data. It was the only report received from Montana this year.)

FALL ON ROCK, INADEQUATE BELAY, MISCOMMUNICATION
Nevada, Red Rocks, American Sportsman
On January 25, 1992, Matt Spydell of Santa Barbara, California, reached the anchors on American Sportsman (5.10c) on the Wall of Confusion, Red Rocks, Nevada. His partner asked if he was off belay, heard what she thought was a yes, and took him off. Spydell leaned back and dropped 40 to 45 feet to the deck. Medivaced to the hospital, he was found to have luckily only fractured a heel.

Analysis
The belayer had not sport climbed much, and expected Spydell to belay or rappel from the top. Usually, sport climbers clip in and are lowered, so you never take them off belay. Also, no one should weight a rope without checking with his belayer. (Source: *Climbing Magazine*, April-May 1992)

FALL ON ICE, FAILURE TO TEST ICE TOOL PLACEMENT, ICE TOOL PULLED OUT, INATTENTION
New Hampshire, Crawford Notch, Hitchcock Gully
On January 9, 1992, my partner, Charles Narnold (22) and I (21) went ice climbing, after spending the night in the AMC hostel in the Notch. We walked down the tracks to the base of Cinema Gully, a moderate ice climb on Mount Willard. The ice in Cinema Gully was generally in good condition with the first pitch being a bit thin. We reached the top around

1200 after about three and a half pitches. After some lunch and a rest, we walked along the tree covered terrace that runs across the face of Mount Willard to the bottom of the final pitch of Hitchcock Gully, another moderate ice climb. Moving into the gully, we set up our belay anchors—two Black Diamond ice screws, and my partner's two tools—and I started up. I found the ice in this gully to be much harder than in the previous climb, probably due to the lack of sun it receives. About ten feet above the belay I stopped to place some protection. While I attempted to clip my ice axe to my harness, my feet slipped. Because my hammer was not placed well enough to catch me, I fell. I snagged my crampons, breaking my left ankle and dislocating my right foot. My partner held my fall and lowered me another 35 to 40 feet down the gully. After making me comfortable and talking for a few minutes, he took off for help, down climbing the rest of the snow and ice to take the railroad tracks.

About two hours after he left, I heard voices and called out so they could find me. The first people to reach me were a climber from the Hostel and an MRS member (Mountain Rescue Service in North Conway, NH). They splinted my legs, put me in a sleeping bag, and lowered me to flatter ground just as the other MRS members arrived. I was put into the litter and lowered the remaining 1500 feet to the tracks where I was put into a sled and dragged to the road. I reached Memorial Hospital in North Conway at 2030, six hours after my fall.

Analysis
The reason for my fall was my poor placement of my ice hammer. When my feet slipped, my hammer broke out of the brittle ice causing me to fall. I should never have attempted to clip my axe until I was sure my hammer was really stuck. Lack of concentration on this easier climb was also a contributory factor. Any time you're on ice with crampons and ice tools, you must be one hundred percent focused on what you're doing. (Source: Joel DePaola)

(Editor's Note: On the same day, two university students from Maine were climbing Hitchcock Gully on Mount Willard when the leader fell and broke his leg. He said if he had known how very brittle and hard the ice was "that day," he would not have tried the route. On the day before, a similar accident occurred on Cathedral Ledge in North Conway. The ice climber fell from Repentance when the brittle ice between his two tools broke, and was compounded when his ice screw protection came out. George Hurley, long-time guide and member of the New Hampshire Mountain Rescue Service, points out that (1) knowledge of the history of the ice formation and (2) learning how to install good protection—in this case equalized screws—are important skills for winter climbers.)

STRANDED—RAPPEL ROPES FROZEN, DARKNESS, INADEQUATE EQUIPMENT
New Hampshire, Cathedral Ledge
On January 28, 1992, two ice climbers (early 20s) got to within about 50 feet of the top of Cathedral Ledge. Because of approaching darkness, they rappelled from a tree growing on the ledge just below the final chimney of Remission. When they tried to pull down their rappel ropes, the ropes moved for about 20 feet and then stuck. The climbers still had both ends of the two rope rappel. They tried for an hour and a half to free the rappel and called for help. Two MRS members went to the top of the cliff. One rappelled to free the ropes which seemed to be frozen in place. The climbers could then make another rappel to the ground.

Analysis
The climbers were not carrying headlamps. With a headlamp, one of them might have been able to prusik up to free the rappel, especially since one of their two ropes was dry, having been in the pack until they started down. The rope they had used for the climb would have had some ice on it, but that rope could have been anchored while one of the climbers ascended the dry rope. However, the climbers were tired, so they were wise not to try a prusik ascent in the dark. They might have avoided the stuck ropes by leaving enough slings to move the rappel anchor point out to the edge of the steep ice. (Source: George Hurley)

FALL FROM RAPPEL, POSSIBLE MISCOMMUNICATION, NO HARD HAT
New Hampshire, Cathedral Ledge
On February 1, 1992, John High (mid 30s) and his partner walked to the top of the north end of Cathedral Ledge and set up both a rappel anchor and a belay anchor on a tree above the ice climb called "The Unicorn," an NEI 4+ which is above the well known rock route "They Died Laughing." John planned to rappel on the two strands of rope which was doubled through the anchor carabiner(s); when he got to a ledge at the bottom of the ice, he was to tug three times on that strand of the rope which was to become his belay rope. His partner was to put that strand into a belay device and then give him a belay as he climbed The Unicorn.

John was killed when he and the rope fell to the bottom of the cliff. Exactly what happened is not known. The partner says that one end of the rope ran quickly through the anchor. One of the first people on the scene, Jim Shimberg, says that the two ends of the rope were still through the figure-of-8 on John's harness when Jim reached him at the bottom of the cliff. These two observations seem to be contradictory.

The partner saw John tie a knot in the ends of the rappel rope. Jim reports that there was no knot when he reached the body. (One end of rope was within several inches of the figure-of-8 and the other end of rope had a few feet to go before it reached the rappel device.)

Analysis
If Jim misinterpreted what he saw when he looked at the rappel device, that is if in fact only one end of rope was still through the device, then John High may have rappelled off one end of his rope and pulled the other end through the anchor. If Jim is correct (and he is sure he is), then possibly John stopped on the ledge below the ice, untied the knot in his rappel rope in preparation for tying one end to his harness, and then fell. If his partner was at the same time preparing to put the rope into a belay device, it is possible that both sides of the rope got into the carabiner so that when the fall occurred, it was in the middle of the rope which ran through the anchor carabiner.

John's method for getting in position for his ice climb was dangerous. A better method would have been to have his partner lower him using a belay device; or, he could have been belayed on one half the rope while rappelling on the other half. (Source: George Hurley)

(Editor's Note: Jim Shimberg's observation from being on the scene indicate a few other problems. First, the communication system they were to use was confusing, especially given that his partner was not an experienced ice climber. Second, the ends of the rope were not tied together. While this did not make a difference in this case, it is an indication *that the victim was not following normal precautions. Another factor that adds to the latter is that he was not wearing a helmet. Third, the system of top-roping he chose was not ordinary. A friend of both the victim and his partner wrote a letter in which she indicated that John High was both knowledgeable and careless. We would agree with her further observation that "careless accidents seem to happen far more frequently to very experienced climbers," and that, "Confidence [can be] dangerous.")*

DISLOCATED KNEE—FALL ON ROCK, MISCOMMUNICATION
New Hampshire, Cathedral Ledge
On July 3, 1992, Mark Chauvin was guiding on Standard and had gone about 35 feet up the Toe Crack to a belay ledge when his first student, who was doing the crux layback move, experienced a dislocated knee and fell as a result. Chauvin did a counter balanced rappel with the student on his back to bring them to the ground. MRS members carried the victim to an ambulance.

Analysis
The student had dislocated his knee before this time. He did not communicate this fact to the guide or to other students. Even though he thought the problem had been corrected, he should have told the guide, and perhaps even have considered wearing an appropriate knee brace. (Source: George Hurley)

FALL ON WET ROCK, NO HARD HAT
New Hampshire, Whitehorse Ledge
On August 2, 1992, Steve Wickham (32) was about 600 feet up on "Wedge" when he fell. His rope was clipped through about six pieces of gear, with the final one being a 1 1/2 Friend which caught his fall of about 50 feet. He was upside down and bleeding profusely, and he was unconscious. The male partner, with a belay from the female, climbed to Steve and righted him. Steve regained consciousness after being out for about seven to ten minutes. He suffered a wound on top of his head, a fractured skull with the break running half way around his head, and two compressed vertebrae.

The accident happened around 1505. The litter-lower rescue by the MRS and other climbers was completed by 1800. Members of SOLO and the North Conway Fire Department Rescue Squad were at the base to carry Steve to the ambulance. Because of the severity of his skull fracture, he was flown from the North Conway Hospital to the Hitchcock Center near Hanover.

Analysis
The victim was not wearing a hard hat. He and his partners had decided that Whitehorse Ledge is a clean cliff, and therefore left helmets in the car. (Source: George Hurley)

FALL ON ROCK, INADEQUATE PROTECTION
New Hampshire, Cathedral Ledge
On October 4, I was climbing at Cathedral Ledge with a friend. We were doing a four pitch 5.9 route called Diedre, and despite the sun, we were on the north side on a cool (but blue) Fall day, which made finger warmth marginal. I was leading the top pitch, a

crack book whose left pages were about one meter wide, and had already reluctantly parted with my #2 Camalot to get to it. At the bottom of the crack, perfectly sized for a #2, as guessed from the base, I had to plant my next largest piece, a #1, far back in said crack. It didn't look too bad, and resisted a few pulls.

I moved up, getting my left foot out on the outside corner and right foot near the crack, to move my left hand up to a high hold near the crack. By the time I'd moved the left foot up and discovered that the only right hand-hold was where the left one was, my left hand was weakening badly. Some combination of it collapsing and my left foot coming off its perch caused me to fall before I was expecting to have to try a retreat. The #1, at waist level, pulled out with no discernible resistance, causing me to go down ten to 12 feet (penduluming a bit) to the next piece (a rap sling), banging the bony protrusion just below and on the outside of my left knee en route and winding up upside down. I quickly righted myself, discovered that I couldn't stand on my left leg, and got lowered back to the ledge. My partner cleaned the pitch with me belaying from a seated position, and rappelled off the sling, then we roped up to move (hop) back down a levelish flake and rappelled to the ground in a single rope-length. After a few failed attempts to hop or walk supported, my partner (5' 6", 130 pounds) carried me the 100 meters down to the road.

The injury proved to be a fracture of the left tibia, requiring a two hour operation and four titanium screws.

Analysis
One's health and fitness are far too valuable to mess with for matters as trivial as poorly placed protection. (Source: Bruce Normand—25)

(Editor's Note: There were a few other incidents of interest in New Hampshire during 1992. In April, a hiker tried to descend Huntington Ravine. He slipped in the fresh show covering hard ice and triggered an avalanche that carried him down 900 feet. He suffered multiple fractures, and was not found until nine hours later. Rescuers got him down. He was wearing work boots and jeans, and had no climbing gear.

Another accident, resulting in a fatality, occurred on Cathedral Ledge in the summer. A young woman (19) was walking with family members on top of Cathedral Ledge when she stumbled on an open slab and fell about 150 feet to the tree covered ledge below the route called "Grim Reaper."

While neither of these is considered to be climbing or mountaineering accidents by our definition, they may be interpreted as such by others, which is unfortunate. It would really be unfortunate if this final description, by George Hurley, were to be categorized as a mountaineering mishap: A 20-year-old from Framingham, Massachusetts, was lost recently for six days on and around Mount Chocorua. During this time he lost his tent and his cigarette lighter (his only fire starter), but otherwise had his camping gear including plenty of food, a sleeping bag, and his battery powered portable TV on which he watched the many searchers and a National Guard helicopter looking for him. If the lost man's explanation is accurate, he did not know what a trail looked like. He expected something grand (like a road), so he crossed trails instead of following them. He also crossed instead of following streams. Had he followed either trails or streams downhill, he would have come to a highway. Instead, he kept moving—mostly uphill—without map or compass or plan until he happened on the Forest Service road which led him out of the woods at the place he went in. His comment after his six days in the woods was, "Great country.")

VARIOUS FALLS ON ROCK, PROTECTION PROBLEMS, PULLING BELAYERS OFF
New York, Mohonk Preserve, Shawangunks
Thirteen accidents were reported in 1992, six of which resulted in fractures—the most serious injuries. In two cases, belayers were pulled from their positions. All but one of the accidents were falls resulting from climbing, including two solo climbers who fell to the ground. One male (47), however, fell because his nut placement demonstration on practice rock above the Uberfall pulled out when he tested it.

One of the reasons attributed to fewer accidents in the area for this year is that there were an unusual number of rain days on the weekends. (Source: Mohonk Preserve)

(Editor's Note: An independent report of a fall from Birdland (5.8), resulting in a severe rope burn behind one knee, came in with an interesting comment. It seems the climber who fell— about 20 feet—tried to hook the rope with his leg and wound up dangling upside down. His partner concluded that, "...a chest harness seems a necessity, especially when climbing where a fall out over an overhang may be realized." This conclusion is not necessarily correct, as research by the French Commission de Securite in Chamonix has shown that free falls with chest harnesses are likely to result in whip-lash injury.)

FALL ON ICE, CLIMBING UNROPED
Oregon, Mount Hood
On February 29, Ralph Leach (40), Tom Morgan (53), and Lee Hepfer (49) successfully ascended the South Side (Hogsback) route on Mount Hood. At 1130 while descending the same route, Hepfer jumped the bergschrund (10,300 feet), slipped, and fell into a fumarole bowl known as "Devil's Kitchen." He was able to self-arrest after sliding about 300 yards. Leach descended to report the accident while Morgan down climbed to assist the injured Hepfer.

A multi-agency (downhill ski patrol, Nordic ski patrol, professional EMT, mountain rescue) hasty team reached the accident site around 1600 and made contact with the two skiers who had just assisted in moving Hepfer to a slightly lower location. A fully equipped Portland Mountain Rescue team left the base at 1637 to support a possible ground evacuation. Hampered by a steep, icy approach and inadequate equipment, two hasty team members managed to reach the subject at 1645. Requests for an air evacuation by the ARRS 304th were met and Hepfer was hoisted aboard a Pavehawk at 1710 and transported to Oregon Health Science University. Hepfer was treated for a broken ankle and lacerations of the face and hand.

Analysis
The bergschrund on the Hogsback is a frequent site for climbing accidents. Numerous climbers have broken or sprained ankles after underestimating the vertical drop of the jump. Down climbing is usually a more controlled and less traumatic maneuver. The use of a rope belay would have prevented the fall. This is particularly prudent if the

snow/ice conditions or climber experience levels do not favor self-arrest. (Source: Jeff Scheetz, Portland Mountain Rescue)

FOOTHOLD DISINTEGRATED, FALL ON ROCK, PROTECTION PULLED OUT, NO HARD HAT
Oregon, Mount Washington
August 16, 1992. The Chimney of Space route begins at a belay stance about 20 feet off the ground. The lead climber (30) led off by ascending a narrow, diagonally upsloping ramp. He used some existing slings and placed other slings over rock horns so there were four placements along the ramp. At the end of the ramp he placed a small camming device and proceeded face climbing up about 10 to 12 feet. He was preparing to place another piece of protection when his toe hold failed and he yelled, "Falling."

He feel feet first, facing the rock, striking the ramp 10 feet below, and sailed backward off into space (head down). About ten feet below the ramp, the rope pulled tight on the fifth piece of protection (the camming device) and it pulled out. The belayer felt very little pull due to rope drag. The leader then continued falling and pendulumed on the fourth piece of protection. It held and the leader's downward fall was arrested, but he then swung (head down) into the rock face below the ramp striking it with his left knee, left elbow, and head. After holding the fall, the belayer called out but received no response. He lowered the leader, who was out of sight, about 15 feet—until slack developed in the rope—and then secured the rope off to the belay anchor before scrambling to where the leader had been lowered.

Due to rope drag, the leader was not on the ground, but was within reach of the belayer who cut the climbing rope and carefully lowered the unconscious climber to the ground. The climber's injuries were assessed and first-aid was administered by the belayer.

The two climbers on the adjacent West Ridge route were made aware of the fall and resulting injuries. They continued to the summit where they came upon a climber with a handheld amateur radio who was able to call for help. An Air Force Reserve rescue team evacuated the injured climber by helicopter.

Analysis
Although I did check the holds, I would certainly do so quite thoroughly in the future—especially in the Cascades. Regardless of comfort level, always be prepared for a hold to give out. The absence of my helmet aggravated the situation as well. This was a bad oversight in preparation. Perhaps I might also have placed protection more frequently. (Source: The climber)

FALL ON ROCK, EXCEEDING ABILITIES, INADEQUATE EQUIPMENT
Oregon, Mount Hood
On October 25, 1992, Terry Beggs (20) and Don Ming (20) started out to "hike" to the summit of Mount Hood. Their clothing consisted of jeans, T-shirts, and work boots. They carried no equipment other than a camera. Just before sunset, the pair reached the base of the Hogsback above Crater Rock and decided to turn back. During the descent, Beggs lost his footing, slipped, and sprained his ankle. They both decided to spend the rest of the night on a rock ledge, sharing one long sleeved shirt between them. Meanwhile, a concerned parent notified the Clackamas County Sheriff's Office of the overdue "hik-

ers." Early on October 26 a multi-agency search was started on the hiking trails near timberline. At 1030 a Portland Mountain Rescue team met the pair descending just west of White River glacier at 7800 feet elevation. The ambulatory subjects were escorted down to Silcox Hut and jeep transported to Timberline Lodge. No medical treatment was required.

Analysis
The two inexperienced, unequipped "day hikers" ignored the posted equipment recommendations and showed a lack of judgment in their attempt to go high on the mountain. Even for an experienced and well equipped party, late season conditions on this volcano make the climb hazardous due to excessive rockfall. (There were five registered parties climbing the South Side route.) The subjects were fortunate that the weather remained fair and unseasonably warm. (Source: Jeff Scheetz)

FALLS ON SNOW, FALLING ROCKS
Oregon, Mount Hood
Following on from the previous report, this summary is presented. Four other accidents involving a combination of falling on snow and falling rocks were reported from Mount Hood from last year. One included a 14 year old boy who slid over a cliff on the south side of the mountain just below Hogsback. He fell 200 yards to his death, and his 12 year old brother, who tried to get to him, was injured in the process as well. Some of the people involved were hikers, some were climbers. Because they were on technical terrain, above timberline, on ice and snow, if an accident occurs, they are considered to be climbing, and are included in the data. (Source: Jed Williamson and various reports from Jeff Scheetz)

EXCEEDING ABILITIES, ASCENDING TOO SLOWLY, EXPOSURE, HYPOTHERMIA, FROSTBITE, WEATHER
Washington, Mount Rainier, Liberty Ridge
About 2000 on May 1, 1992, the park received a message from the emergency radio located at Camp Muir from the summit. The climber, Shannon Stegg (26) was hypothermic, incoherent, and had frostbite. He reported that his climbing partner, Jerry Roberts (26), had left him on the summit the night before and had gone to get help. Two rangers left for Camp Muir and brought Stegg to Paradise the following morning. They learned from Stegg that Roberts had left the summit the evening of April 30 to get help for Stegg, who was suffering from hypothermia. A search was started for Roberts with aircraft and ground personnel. Search teams were placed on all descent routes. Two helicopters were brought in and an aerial search began. The light commercial helicopter found tracks leading down from the summit on the Tahoma Glacier. A military chinook helicopter moved search personnel into position where the tracks entered the trees. By use of ground personnel with helicopter support, Rogers was found. He was totally exhausted, hungry, and suffered from frostbite. There appeared to be no permanent damage.

The search involved two helicopters, 12 volunteers from Tacoma and Seattle Mountain Rescue Councils, two guides from RMI and at least ten park personnel. (Source: William A. Larean, Ranger, Mount Rainier National Park)

Analysis
In an interview with Shannon Stegg, the following information was obtained.

Stegg and Roberts had planned to ascend Mount Rainier from April 23 through April 29, 1992. Their chosen route was to enter from Carbon River and Ascend via the Carbon Glacier. Once atop the summit, they would continue down to either Camp Schurman via Emmons Glacier or to Camp Muir via Gibraltar Rock.

Stegg had successfully climbed in or on the following areas or peaks: The Andromeda Strain, North Face of Mount Temple, and the Patagonia region. Stegg believed Roberts to be the premiere rock climber in the State of Georgia, and known by Stegg to have climbed in the Tetons. Stegg considered Roberts to be in better physical condition.

They arrived in Seattle on April 22, intent on climbing Rainier, in preparation for an ascent of Denali in May. They were surprised to find the Carbon River Area closed. Their route took them across the Carbon Glacier where they cached their cross country skis. They approached the summit via Liberty Ridge. Stegg recalled Roberts saying that he wasn't comfortable in climbing in this terrain, and that Stegg should plan on going alone to rendezvous with the other team awaiting them at Denali. Stegg said there was four days of food between them that could stretch to eight if needed.

They climbed to within 400 yards of the summit in good weather. While there, a storm arrived. The storm lasted three days. Several feet of snow was deposited around and on their tent. Stegg recalled having spent two hours outside attempting to clear the snow away from the tent. He became very chilled and began to notice the onset of hypothermia. The snow had rendered the tent useless.

Roberts had led Stegg to the summit, in search of steam vents they'd read existed. Stegg's eyes had frozen almost closed, he said he could just make out Roberts' shadow. Roberts found a small steam vent for Stegg to spend the night. After fixing Stegg some hot drink, Roberts began to plan a descent to get help for Stegg. Stegg was in a full shiver and very weak.

Stegg did recall Roberts studying a route down Emmons Glacier toward Camp Schurman. Stegg tried to talk Roberts out of leaving, in fear that Roberts might not be able to make it down with just a sleeping bag, a powerbar and some cheese for food. Stegg wished Roberts good luck and Roberts was off.

Stegg saw blue sky later that evening. The following morning he felt good enough to search the crater for Roberts, not seeing any sign of him. Believing he could not survive another night on the summit, he began to descend toward Camp Muir, remembering he'd been there previously. He successfully reached Camp Muir. A climbing team fixed him soup and helped him raise help via the emergency radio.

Roberts was interviewed by Plans Chief Wilcox and others at the Kautz Creek heliport, including rangers Larson, Winslow Brooks, and Kirschner. Some information provided by Roberts differed somewhat from that given by Stegg during his interview earlier in the day. Major remarks by Roberts during the interview include the following:

Roberts was very concerned about the physical well being of his climbing partner, because Stegg was suffering from both hypothermia and frostbite. Roberts said that his own condition was good. Roberts felt that he needed to get to Camp Muir to get help for Stegg. When Roberts left Stegg in a steam cave on the north side of the east crater, near Columbia Crest itself, on the late afternoon of April 30, he wandered around the summit crater system until he found a large steam cave near the southwestern part of the crater where he then spent the night.

At daybreak on May 1, Roberts left the summit crater and started down climbing the upper Nisqually Glacier with the intention of going to Camp Muir for help. Neither he nor Stegg was aware of the usual descent route to Camp Muir. They thought the descent was somewhere near Gibraltar Rock, so Roberts headed in that direction. He said he could see Paradise, as the weather was clear and not excessively windy, and he headed generally in that direction. This direction resulted in his going west of Gibraltar Rock to the top of the Nisqually Ice Cliff system, which he recognized as something he could not descend. Because Roberts could see no safe way of descending to Camp Muir, or Paradise, he decided to climb back up toward the summit and descend to Camp Schurman via the Emmons Glacier instead. Despite having good weather conditions, Roberts readily admitted he had none of the essential ingredients for a safe descent: he was alone and unroped, he had no map, no compass, and no knowledge of the descent route to either Camp Muir or Camp Schurman. As a result, he mistakenly thought that by climbing back toward the col between the two summits he could see (Point Success and Columbia Crest), he could descend over the other side to Camp Schurman. He climbed through the saddle between these summits and descended the Tahoma Glacier (instead of the Emmons, as intended) down the "sickle" area, and continued down the major portion of the Tahoma Glacier. Roberts said that he encountered many dangers, walking over snow bridges that spanned crevasses ("crevices," as he termed them) and in some cases descending into and back out of larger and wider crevasse systems. Ultimately he traversed southwesterly across the middle portions of both the Tahoma and South Tahoma Glaciers and reached solid ground on the lower Success Cleaver area around the 8,000 foot level. He then descended snow covered slopes northeast of Pyramid Peak and into Pyramid Park. Shortly after entering the solid forest just west of Pearl Falls, he bivouacked for the night.

The next morning, May 2, Roberts continued his descent down wooded slopes and followed an unnamed stream just west of Pearl Creek until it joined Pearl Creek near the valley bottom at the 4,300 foot level. He then walked a short distance further southwest until he reached Kautz Creek, the glacial river and primary drainage in the valley. Roberts followed Kautz Creek downstream, hoping that it would eventually lead to a road but not realizing where he was. By mid to late morning, he arrived at the Wonderland Trail, where the trail crosses Kautz Creek. Roberts said that he began to follow the trail to the "left" (toward Longmire) but became discouraged because the trail was climbing back uphill and seemed to be leading him in the wrong direction. He elected, instead, to continue following Kautz Creek downhill. As Roberts followed the river down the valley, he heard helicopters flying above him and toward the mountain.

He reasoned that they were attempting to rescue Stegg, whom Roberts thought would likely still be on the summit. Stegg had long since climbed on his own to Camp Muir, contacted rangers, was interviewed and taken to Good Samaritan Hospital for treatment of frostbite.

Finally, shortly after 1500, Roberts was spotted by Ranger Olson in the military Chinook helicopter as Roberts was walking along the river at the 3,000 foot elevation. This is approximately 1.25 miles downstream from the Wonderland Trail Crossing and about 1.75 miles above the Kautz Trail crossing. A Bell 206B III helicopter with Ranger Winslow aboard was able to come to the scene, land nearby and fly Roberts to the Kautz Creek heliport. Roberts was provided food and drink, was interviewed, and driven to Good Samaritan Hospital for treatment of some frostbite on two fingers. (Source: J. Wilcox, Ranger, Mount Rainier National Park)

FALL ON ROCK, PROTECTION PULLED OUT, OVERCONFIDENT
Washington, Peshastin Pinnacles, Orchard Rock
On May 15, 1992, I was teaching an inexperienced climber the proper use of protection. I was on sandstone with few places for placing protection. I had climbed 25 feet, then put in two pieces, then told my belayer that I was falling. I then jumped off the rock face. A moment later, I heard a noise, looked behind me, and saw my protection had failed. I hit the ground, resulting in abrasions, lacerations, and a fractured leg. I was wearing a helmet, and I believe it saved my life.

Analysis
My analysis of this accident is overconfidence. I have been climbing for over 20 years, taught as a paid instructor, put up many new routes, climbed many of the hard routes in the States. It is embarrassing to think that I could become so careless. (Source: Steve Baker—35)

FALL ON ROCK, PLACED INADEQUATE PROTECTION, OUT OF PRACTICE
Washington, Snoqualmie Pass, Chair Peak
My son Erik Podenski (14) and I (42) were climbing the Northeast Buttress route on Chair Peak on May 16, 1992. This route is rated Class 4. I led all the rock pitches. We had completed the crooked chimney pitch and proceeded up the ridge to a shallow rock basin. There we ascended leftward toward a small patch of trees. The basin is generally Class 2 or 3 until the final 30+ feet below the tree pitch.

I placed a runner on the only available rock horn before starting up the last section. However, this left me approximately 60+ feet above the horn at the point where I fell. I was trying to traverse left to a point where I could get above the basin near the tree patch. I attempted to traverse to a hold to my left, keeping my right hand and foot stationary, while moving my left foot and left hand toward the hold. My right foot slipped and I took a tumbling/sliding fall down to where the basin was less steep. The total distance traveled was about 120 feet on a grade which was possibly 65 degrees at the top and around 25 degrees at the bottom.

My injuries consisted of three broken ribs, numerous abrasions, a cut on the left hand requiring five stitches, a cut on the back of the head requiring several stitches, and an extensive bruise on the left thigh and buttock. In addition, I was quite chilled even though it was a moderately nice day. At the time we reached the top of the crooked chimney, we met two climbers who were descending the Northeast Buttress route. At the time of the fall I yelled quite loudly. By this time the other two climbers were at the summit base slopes. These climbers heard me yell and yelled back, asking if we needed a rescue. My son answered yes and the two climbers proceeded back to the Alpental parking lot which is at the head of the trail. I haven't seen these two climbers since, but would like to thank them for their help.

We were airlifted off Chair Peak by an Army helicopter rescue team one at a time. I was then flown to Harborview Trauma Center in Seattle. The air rescue took place approximately 2 1/2 hours after the accident. This timely response was due to the two climbers who were on Chair Peak. I feel very grateful to the Army crewman who performed the rescue as well as the two climbers.

Analysis

I had climbed this same route twice previously without any difficulty. However, those two occasions were in 1980-1981. During the early 80s I was quite active in rock climbing, including many Class 5 climbs. At the time of the accident, I had not done any serious rock climbing in several years.

It was customary for me in the past to do an annual re-familiarization with rock climbing, starting on practice areas such as Mount Erie and only then climbing in the mountains. However, prior to the accident, I did not do this in 1992. Because my wife and I have twin baby girls at home, I had very little time to get out climbing and this absence of re-familiarization and practice undoubtedly contributed to my accident.

Because my son was getting very interested in climbing and had shown a good deal of natural talent as a climber, I was somewhat swayed to go out with him. I felt that because the route was one that I had done twice previously (and I didn't recall any difficulties) that I would be up to the challenge. This seemed to be the case for me when I was able to easily do the main Class 4 pitch up the chimney.

By the time that I got to the basin where I fell, I was somewhat tired, but not exhausted. However, being somewhat tired may have affected my judgment. In retrospect I felt that I should not have been making a traversing move with only one hand and one foot fixed. A three point stance would have provided better stability.

One other contributing factor was the shoes that I was wearing. I had on a pair of low cut Vasque hiking shoes which have a Vibram look-alike compound rubber sole. However, the instep area of the shoe is not very good and I have previously slipped on trails and other places when side-stepping with these shoes.

In summary, I believe that this accident was preventable. The most important factor would have been to go out and do the standard re-familiarization/practice sessions prior to going in the mountains. From a mental standpoint, I was overconfident because of my previous experiences climbing Chair Peak, although these did not reconcile with my lack of recency in rock climbing experience. (Source: Patrick Podenski)

FALL ON ROCK, PROTECTION PULLED OUT, PLACED INADEQUATE PROTECTION, NO HARD HAT
Washington, Peshastin Pinnacles, Lightning Crack

On May 31, 1992, Bob Renz (40) was climbing Lightning Crack. He placed protection at the beginning of the climb and then didn't place protection when the crack was not as steep and difficult to climb. When he reached the crux of the climb, approximately 70 feet off the ground, he placed a cam and stopper, and then fell just above these two pieces of protection. Neither piece held his fall and were ripped right out of the sandstone. He fell all the way to the ground, smashing into the rock several times as he fell, and then sliding the remaining distance to the ground. He sustained severe head injuries, broken leg and smashed knee cap— all as he bounced against rock as he fell.

Analysis

Wear a helmet at all times—top rope climbing, belaying, leading or just hanging out at base of rock when there is potential of rock fall. Even at "sport climbing" area such as Peshastin Pinnacles.

Be aware of the type of rock you are placing protection in. Sometimes even the best placed protection will not hold a fall in sandstone.

Watch spacing of protection in relation to grounding out if leader falls, or if piece of protection fails, whether or not another piece of protection will be able to prevent the climber from falling to the ground. (Source: Lesa Duncan)

FALLING ROCK DISLODGED BY CLIMBER
Washington, Mount Shuksan, Fisher Chimneys

On June 20, 1992, Bill Peterson (33) was descending the Fisher Chimneys and was about 200 feet above the base of the summit block when he was struck by a large rock dislodged from above. He fell 20 feet, landed on his pack and helmet (on his head), fell another 20 feet coming to rest on snow and rock. He sustained bruises and minor cuts, and was able to descend on his own along with the rest of the party of six.

Analysis

There is serious rockfall danger on the summit pyramid. A more severe injury was barely avoided. It is a bad idea for students to carry heavy packs in the chimney. (Source: Greg Starling and Tom Whitney, Leader and Assistant Leader of this climb)

FALL ON ROCK, PLACED INADEQUATE PROTECTION, PROTECTION PULLED OUT
Washington, Stuart Range, Colchuck Peak

On June 21, 1992, Kevin Coplin (36) and Allan G. Fries (46), two experienced climbers, fell to their death while ascending Colchuck Peak. What follows is a report from a member of the search parties that recovered the bodies.

Because the identity of the climbers was not defined to me at the time, I will refer to them as Climber A and Climber B. I believe that Climber A is Fries and B is Coplin from information given by friends (or family) at the Chelan County heliport following the retrieval.

We had been told by the reporting party that the climbers were on the Serpentine Arete on Dragontail peak and that one was a competent 5.9 climber; the other climbed at 5.7. We conducted a thorough search of Dragontail, including this route and all moats at its base. During the day, we were radioed additional information that they might be on "something with ten pitches of 5.9." We looked at other routes on Dragontail and searched the Northeast Buttress of Colchuck Peak with binoculars. (This route had just been described in a climbing magazine as a Northwest classic!) We observed a party on that route and decided that if the missing people were on the Northeast Buttress, they would see them. We did search one bergschrund at the base of the Northeast Couloir.

The climbers were located in the moat between Colchuck Glacier and the peak directly under the Northeast Buttress route. The moat was approximately 15 feet wide and Climber A was about 25 feet down on a snow ledge. He was wearing a large fanny pack (est. 15 pounds) and had a typical rock rack, including nuts and camming devices. The rope from his harness was tied to a halftwist type locking carabiner with a clove hitch. The 'biner was clipped to a two inch camming device. The rope was threaded through a belay plate to a carabiner on his harness. Only a short length of the rope was between the belay plate and the anchor. There was approximately 125 feet between Climber A and Climber B.

Climber B was some ten feet lower in the moat (in a much more narrow section) and essentially immediately below A. He was wearing a large rucksack (est. 35 pounds) and had a few nuts and other hardware on his harness. There was one small wired nut loose on the snow in the moat; it did not have a carabiner or sling on it. There were no slings, carabiners, or other protection clipped to the rope between climbers.

Based on these observations, we proposed the following scenario to explain the accident. The climbers had completed the first several difficult (up to 5.8) pitches and reached a "huge left-slanting ledge." Beckey's guide indicates that the ledge is easy, has some trees, and is 160 feet long. We believe that Climber A led across the ledge placing no protection, and established his belay with the single two inch cam. Climber B removed his belay anchor (the few pieces on his harness) and proceeded across the ledge. His 125 foot fall was held by A's belay plate, but the single anchor failed to hold Climber A. Because of his head and neck injuries, B may have been killed by the pendulum fall. Both climbers went straight down into the moat, with A landing above B. The loose wired nut with the bodies may have been A's attempt to get something else in when the fall occurred, or may have been a piece that B had just removed. The fact that it did not have a carabiner tends to indicate the former.

Analysis
A number of points were made. If one is not going to climb the route that was originally signed out, then leave a note in base camp as to where one decided to go. Had they not died instantly, they would most certainly have died of exposure in the ensuing ten days, because no one knew where to look. This route is known by many others to be very unstable and unsafe in its first pitches because of loose, "rotten pink rock," as stated in Beckey's guidebook. Never climb more than a few feet above a belayer without putting in at least one piece of protection, preferably more; one piece might have saved both of them. Wear a helmet, though in this case it probably would not have helped; it almost certainly would have had they used some protection for the lead climber. Belay anchors should be more than one piece when warranted. The second climber should be protected on a traverse. (A few slings around the trees would have resulted in a short fall instead of 125 feet here.) (Source: Freeman Keller, Chelan County Mountain Rescue, and Dr. Michael Brown)

FALL ON SNOW, INADEQUATE PROTECTION, FALL INTO CREVASSE, HYPOTHERMIA, NO ICE AXES USED TO PREVENT ROPE CUTTING THROUGH SNOW
Washington, Mount Shuksan, Fisher Chimneys
On July 7, 1992, at 1600, a nine person party was descending Mount Shuksan via Hell's Highway, a steep transitional section from the Sulphide Glacier to the Curtis Glacier. The middle person, Silvia Cate (38) of the second rope team, lost her footing in very soft snow and began sliding toward a large crevasse approximately 60 feet downslope. Ms. Cate tried to affect self-arrest but she could not get the ice axe to find purchase in the soft snow and slush. Ms. Cate pulled the other two rope team members off their feet and they also began sliding toward the crevasse.

Despite their efforts, the other two rope team members could not self-arrest and were heading for the crevasse. Ms. Cate fell approximately 35 feet into the crevasse becoming wedged in tightly between the ice walls and covered with loose, wet snow.

Her other partner, the lead on the rope team, Katie Foehl (48), fell into the crevasse approximately 50 feet down from the lip and was tightly wedged in between the ice walls. The third member of the rope team, Candy Morgan, slid over the open crevasse and landed on the downhill side of the crevasse and managed to stabilize herself in that location.

The next sequence of events is difficult to follow. Here is what has been recalled. Apparently the remaining seven members contacted another party in the same area to request assistance. This group had a Marine transceiver with them. They contacted Vancouver Coast Guard on Marine Channel 24, who relayed the distress message to the Vancouver Marine Operator, who contacted the Glacier Public Service Center (US Forest Service HWY 542), who then contacted Marblemount Ranger Station.

The remaining members affected the extrication of the two climbers. A system was set up to haul Ms. Cate out of the crevasse. They managed to raise her to within 15 feet of the lip of the crevasse. At this point the rope had cut through the snow and ice to a depth of three to four feet and became jammed. No chafing gear (ice axes or padding) was set up to insure a free running rope.

At this time, another climbing party came on scene as they were descending the same route. They assisted the party in trouble, set up another raising system and lowered another rope to Ms. Cate, who was 15 feet below the lip. Ms. Cate was then free and clear of the crevasse and attended to by the people in her party. It is estimated that she was in the crevasse for 45 minutes. She was thoroughly chilled and had her clothing changed out by other members of the party.

The rescuers then attempted to raise Katie Foehl out of the crevasse. She was stuck hard between the ice walls. The assisting climbing party had set up a raising system on the upslope side of the crevasse; the other system was ineffective because the rope was cutting into the snow. Katie was stuck so hard that Brad Rodgers was lowered into the crevasse to free Katie. He was belayed with ice screws on the upslope side of the crevasse. Brad cut the pack straps on Katie's pack to help free her up. Rescuers above began hauling her up and Brad stemmed up the ice walls and assisted in yarding her up. Katie was in the crevasse approximately two hours.

At 1855, Highline Helicopter with NPS SAR personnel departed Marblemount with rescue personnel. On scene at 1925, helicopter was able to land just below the crevasse. Both climbers were out and were attended to by fellow climbers. The victims were suffering early to advanced stages of hypothermia, but no other serious injuries noted. (Source: Uwe Nehring, Ranger, Mount Rainier National Park)

Analysis
There was too much slack in the rope between Katie, Syl and Candy. The slope should have been protected either via leapfrogging or pickets (which the party did not have). Syl continued to slide, gaining momentum. Observation (based on subsequent conversation with Katie): Syl should have yelled, "Falling," as Katie was unaware of what was happening until she was pulled off her feet. I believe Candy went into self-arrest immediately, as did Katie once she was pulled, but the slope angle, speed and snow conditions did not allow for self-arrest.

The effectiveness of the arrest, especially since I had my pick fairly close to my right hip and quite a bit of my body weight over it. In firmer snow I think I might have been able to stop myself. I remember zipping past a crevasse or two—I am not sure if I went by them or over them. I just have a vague, visual image of flying past them while trying to self-arrest. The next thing I knew I went over the lip of the crevasse—flipping so that I was falling back first, head leading.

(What follows next are some additional excerpts from Sylvia Cate's eight page description of her two hour ordeal in the crevasse.)

I remember every inch of the fall vividly. Part of my brain realized that I was falling very likely to my death; part of my brain was processing how pretty it all was, especially the clumps of snow exploding against the ice walls as I fell. I kept expecting the rope to come taut and stop me, but I continued to fall, narrowly missing an ice tower, snow exploding everywhere, the bright blue sky and sunlight getting further and further away until, Wham! I stopped—wedged tight at about a (I estimate) 45 degree angle, feet above, head below, staring straight up at the sky and sunlit ice walls at the lip, and then, whoomp! All the pretty exploding snow landed on top of my chest and face, completely filling my nose and mouth so I could not breathe. I was pretty sure I was going to die by suffocation. Fortunately I had use of part of my left arm and I was able to dig the snow out and start breathing again. I was dry retching and gasping for air when another huge clump of snow fell, suffocating me again. I was now convinced I was going to die. I dug out the snow again from my mouth and nose—amazed at how tightly it was packed in. I think once I caught my breath again I began screaming hysterically for help. A bit of confusion—a lot of voices—echoing off the walls….

I can see my watch—it's about 4:15-4:20 or so. I'm pretty sure I'm going to die— probably of hypothermia—before (if) I get pulled out. In between waves of total hysterical panic during which I kept screaming to Howard to hurry, I talk to Katie some. She's wedged. She's been able to loosen her chin strap so she can breathe some. We both cycle through periods of panic screaming—generally hollering, "Hurry and please get us out." Howard keeps telling us, "We're working on it; don't worry, we'll get you out." I know he's working on it and I know they're all hurrying as fast as safety allows. I try hard not to holler because I don't want to distract them. But I'm also getting so cold, it's hard not to go into a screaming frenzy. I have told Howard Katie's status and I hear him tell the folks on top to concentrate on Katie first. I keep looking at my watch to keep myself focused. I know it's going to take time. I have to hang on…

Another tug. I must be 12 to 15 feet below the lip, and I see the rope has sawed through all the soft snow at the edge— probably has cut through at least three to four feet. Malcom's head pops over. I can see he's in the sun and I'm so envious. I want out, now. He asks me if I can use my prusiks to get out. Ha! The rope at my harness tie-in is still a confusing jumble wrapped around prusiks and one another, and besides, I can't use my hands. I stare at them and wonder stupidly why they're so white. I explain to Malcom I can't do it. He lowers a second rope to me with a little stiff sack tied to it—gloves inside! It takes me a good five minutes to get them on—I'm so cold. I think they're still expecting me to prusik out. I know I can't Even if I can get my hands to work again, I'm shivering too violently and I'm too weak. I get an idea. I see the problem with the rope cutting through the lip. I ask them to give me a bit of slack—they lower me about a foot to a little snow bridge. Somehow I manage to snag a 'biner off my rack and clip the second rope to my harness. "Pull me up on this one," I say. I keep trying to kick steps into the soft snow at the lip to help myself out, but it just crumbles away. I am so close to blue sky and sunlight and Malcom and maybe warmth, but it doesn't matter. I'm shaking violently—I can't get my hands to work and I'm just kicking more and more snow down. Thank God it wasn't falling on Katie. A tug. They're pulling me up with the second rope—as I get closer, Malcom and Don lean over and horse me out over the lip.

FALL WHILE DESCENDING, OFF ROUTE, INADEQUATE EXPERIENCE, ETC.
West Virginia, Judy Gap Rocks

On February 28, 1992, David Dugan (42), Dean Beal (36), Belinda Smith, and her son (10) set out to attempt climbs on some obvious rock pinnacles on the north side of Judy Gap, about 15 miles south of Seneca Rocks. (All are Grade 5, and although the rocks are not frequently climbed, various of the rescuers had climbed the pinnacles and faces over the last two decades.) There are a lot of loose rocks and slick footing, even in dry conditions. The formation is the same Tuscarora Sand that comprises Seneca Rocks and both the approach and the rock are similar. Weather was breezy, clear, and sub-freezing; there was no snow on the ground and the leaves were quite dry. The area is brushy and steep up to the exposed rock of the ridgetop.

The four had gotten into rock more difficult than they liked and turned back, missed their ascent route and pushed downward. Beal and Smith passed into the main descent gully, but Dugan and the youngster found themselves atop a system of brushy, sloped ledges and drops. Dugan tied the boy in (but not himself) and gave him an over the shoulder belay to the next ledge. When the rope went slightly slack, Dugan leaned over the edge to see whether the boy had made it down. (They didn't have a call system.) The boy at that moment dropped the last foot, jerking Dugan in a complete flip down about 15 feet to the same ledge. He missed the boy.

Dugan landed on his right leg and then his hip. This ledge was also steeply sloped and buried in leaves, but he snagged on some brush and managed to stop his slide. Injuries were a broken right ankle and pain in the lower back/hip area. Beal descended to the van to send for the Rescue Squad and the State Police (about 1700) then returned with blankets. The father and two sons at the next farm were EMTs on the North Fork Squad, so response to the victim was fast. The guide school at Seneca Rocks and the Tactical Skills Team at Franklin were notified soon after and a team was fielded by 1800 in approaching darkness. In addition to his injuries, the victim was becoming hypothermic by the time rescuers arrived. Lowering the victim through the remaining ledges began about 1930; he came across the last steep gully on a high line about 2130.

Injuries were later determined to be a fractured right distal fibular epiphysis (ankle injury), compressed L1 vertebra, and massive abdominal bruising without internal organ injury.

Analysis

It is not unusual hereabouts to hear someone claim that they "climb a lot," meaning what climbers would call scrambling; and while the great faces of Seneca do not normally attract scramblers, smaller rocks do. It's very easy, especially on descent among the ledges, to get beyond your skill and equipment levels. The rock faces around Pendleton County are deceptive; they are often covered with lots of brush and do not look very steep from a distance. However, the ledges are usually outsloping and covered thickly with old leaves, the brush is not securely rooted, and the faces between ledges are often unexpectedly high. Scramblers often do not perceive the true danger involved because the ground does not feel especially steep. Route finding down ledges is difficult even if you've been studying the return route during ascent.

In this case, the "climbers" had one carabiner and a 20 foot length of nylon clothesline. Dugan had a homemade seat harness with attached pack. They were dressed in basic outdoor clothes with lace up smooth-soled work boots of several kinds. Dugan said he and Beal had "climbed quite a bit" and that Belinda and her son had joined them for some easy scrambling to the top of the ridge.

In an interview at the hospital two days later, Dugan said he'd been climbing since he was 17 years old, first in the Catskills, later in the Adirondacks, and more recently in the Shenandoah National Park. (But he'd never heard of the Gunks, of known climbs in northern New York, and only recently had he heard of Seneca Rocks.) His preference in climbing rope runs to surplus military rappel (static) line and not much other gear, though he's been working on a combination seat harness/rucksack. He's a skydiver but said he can't see sense in spending money on climbing gear. (Source: Jim Underwood, Tactical Skills Team, Franklin, WV)

(Editor's Note: Unfortunately, this is one of those cases that can be picked up by the media, National Safety Council, federal and state agencies, etc., as an example of how dangerous the sport is—and how incompetent the participants are.)

FALL ON SNOW, OFF ROUTE, INEXPERIENCED
Wyoming, Grand Teton National Park, Middle Teton
On May 30, 1992, a climber (20) and his partner were on the way down what they thought was the Southwest Couloir of the Middle Teton, at 1630 and fell about 800 feet down a steep snow slope and over two 40 to 50 foot cliff bands. Both are unclear if the two to four foot avalanche debris they were caught in was started by the fall or caused the fall. Arms was unconscious for about five minutes after the fall and had a fractured heel. Walter went to Garnet Meadows to get their tent and sleeping bags which he used to stabilize Arms before Arms was flown out by NPS helicopter at 0800 on May 31, and was taken to St. John's Hospital where he was treated for a fractured talus.

Analysis
The pillow of snow around Arms and the fact that he was wearing a helmet probably saved his life. He told ranger Springer he remembers hitting his head several times during the fall. The climbers' relative inexperience, lack of route finding skills, and soft snow conditions probably caused this accident. (Source: Scott Berkenfield, SAR Ranger, Grand Teton National Park)

LOSS OF CONTROL—VOLUNTARY GLISSADE
Wyoming, Grand Teton National Park, Owen Couloir
On June 9, 1992, H. Kammeyer (33) and his partner departed from a high camp at the Lower Saddle for an ascent of the complete Exum Ridge route on the Grand Teton. They completed the route, reaching the summit of the Grand around 1200. They then successfully descended to the Upper Saddle.

Both then started down the standard descent in the Owen Couloir below the Upper Saddle. Kammeyer elected to descend the snow in the couloir while his partner descended a rock rib. The snow near the top of the couloir was described by Kammeyer as being soft and wet.

Kammeyer passed his partner in a sitting glissade. He watched as Kammeyer appeared to accelerate in his glissade about 50 yards below the Upper Saddle. He approached a cliff band in the couloir about 100 feet high and attempted to use his ice axe to self-arrest, by putting the pick of his axe into the snow with only one hand gripping the shaft of the axe. The ice axe was ripped out of his hand and he cartwheeled several times before falling over the lip of the cliff band and out of sight of his partner.

With no visual or voice contact with the victim, the partner continued down the standard descent. After 25 minutes, he saw Kammeyer lying motionless on the snow about 100 feet above the Black Dike. He had fallen down the mixed snow and rock for a vertical distance of about 800 feet. After another five minutes or so, the partner reached Kammeyer.

The partner reported that he initially examined the victim and found him to be confused, disoriented and did not know who his partner was. He appeared to have sustained two broken arms, a head injury and possible rib fractures. He was conscious, however, and was able to stand since he did not appear to have injured his legs. Remarkably, the partner was able to assist Kammeyer down to their camp at the Lower Saddle. Upon reaching camp, he put his partner in a sleeping bag in their tent and enlisted the help of other climbers at the Saddle.

The partner left the Lower Saddle at 1620 to descend Garnet Canyon and report the accident. At 1730, he met ranger Larson on the Garnet trail as Larson was descending from a mountain patrol of Irene's Arete. Larson reported the incident via radio. At 1732, I requested dispatch of the park contract helicopter. It landed at Lupine Meadows at 1824. The helicopter landed on the Lower Saddle and ranger personnel reached the victim at 1839.

Ranger personnel evaluated and stabilized Kammeyer with C-collar and backboard, assisted by a physician who happened to be in the area. They then initiated a carry of the patient from his camp to the helispot. At 1929, the helicopter, with the victim and Ranger Dorward on board, left the Saddle for a direct flight to St. John's Hospital in Jackson, arriving there at 1937.

Kammeyer was reported to have sustained: bilateral wrist fractures, a right side pneumothorax, and fractures of T-8, T-12 and C4-7.

Analysis
Kammeyer was wearing a climbing helmet at the time of his fall. The helmet was extensively damaged in the fall and quite probably saved his life or prevented an even worse head injury. The cause of the accident was an inability to self-arrest on snow due to improper technique. It was subsequently reported that prior to the accident, the wrist loop on the ice axe was broken. The partner indicated that earlier in the day Kammeyer had demonstrated proper self-arrest technique as they approached the climb. But at a critical moment when it most counted, he was unable to execute a self-arrest. (Source: Peter Armington, SAR Ranger, Grand Teton National Park)

PITON PULLED OUT, FALL ON ROCK, REMOVED PROTECTION
Wyoming, Grand Teton National Park, Guides' Wall
On June 26, 1992, at 1145, Roland Fleck (59) was leading the "Flake Pitch" on the regular Guides' Wall route belayed by partner Wes Mostaert. This pitch is about 500 feet off the ground and is considered to be 5.7 in difficulty. After clipping into a fixed piton, Fleck apparently then reached down and removed two other pieces of protection that he himself had placed. He body weighted the piton, applying an outward force to it at which point it suddenly pulled out of the rock. He fell 40 to 50 feet down to the ledge at the base of the pitch and sustained multiple injuries upon impact. Mostaert

moved him into as stable a position as he could and began calling for help.

The Park dispatch office received a report of an accident in Cascade Canyon around 1343 and, at the time, a specific location was not known. Ranger Jim Dorward, who was just below the Forks area, ran 2.5 miles down the trail where a more precise report had led him to believe the accident was in the vicinity of Guides' Wall. This popular rock climb is six pitches in length and is located on the lower southwest ridge of Storm Point. Dorward very quickly ascended what is the normal descent route to a point from which he could traverse a ledge to the accident site. This involved climbing nearly 1,000 vertical feet. He began an initial patient assessment at 1455.

By 1550, a helicopter departed Lupine Meadows for the accident scene. The short-haul litter and the medical and climbing equipment that it contained was delivered to the accident site. Ranger Dorward placed Fleck carefully into the litter on his injured side while the helicopter orbited nearby. Eight minutes later, Dorward successfully attached the litter to the end of the short-haul ropes. The weather at that time was quite bad with 15 mph winds and steady rain. Pilot Will Eldredge managed to accomplish this very tricky maneuver with a main rotor clearance of ten feet. After a flight of four minutes, Fleck was taken into the rescue cache and briefly tended by an air ambulance flight nurse. He was then quickly reloaded into the helicopter and flown directly to St. John's Hospital in Jackson, arriving at 1700, where he received initial treatment. Due to the serious nature of Fleck's multiple injuries, he was flown to the Shock Trauma unit of the LDS hospital in Salt Lake City at 2130.

Analysis

It is unfortunate that Fleck decided to remove two pieces of protection and then put all of his trust in one old, presumably untested, piton.

The rescue itself was one of the most technical short-haul operations yet undertaken in Grand Teton National Park. The speed with which Ranger Jim Dorward climbed safely to the scene, the flying skills and bravery of pilot Will Eldredge and the spotting ability of Ranger Steve Rickert all combined into an effort that was nothing short of heroic. That this was done during very adverse weather conditions is nothing less than astonishing. The application of the short-haul technique has most certainly revolutionized mountain rescue in Grand Teton. (Source: Peter Armington, SAR Ranger, Grand Teton National Park)

FALL ON SNOW, UNABLE TO SELF-ARREST, INEXPERIENCED
Wyoming, Grand Teton National Park, Mount Teewinot

On July 10, 1992, at 1050, a victim slipped and fell while attempting an ascent of the east face of Teewinot. She and her partner were at the 11,800 foot level near the bottom of the snow-filled couloir that leads to the summit of the peak, just 500 feet above. She lost her footing on the snow, slid for 30 feet and then somersaulted into the talus where she came to rest just slightly above a large cliff. Her climbing partner managed to move her into a stable, sitting position and then started passing the word down the mountain that a rescue was needed. There were four other parties on the face at the time of the accident.

The accident was reported at the Jenny Lake Ranger Station at 1200, and the Aerospatiale Lama was requested from Yellowstone. Due to the longer response time of this helicopter, rangers Larson and Carr were dispatched on foot from the Lupine Meadows parking area at 1215. Upon arrival of the Lama at 1325, rangers Harrington, Irvine and Dorward were flown to the 11,500 foot saddle on the west side of the mountain with medical gear and limited climbing equipment. Larson was first on the accident scene at 1426 and began an initial patient assessment shortly afterward. She was reported to be in stable condition with possible injuries to her head, lower back and arm.

A decision to short-haul the patient was made and the helicopter was rigged for the operation. The short-haul litter and additional equipment was delivered at 1520 and the patient was placed on a backboard. The hook-up procedure was completed at 1552 and the patient arrived back down at the Lupine Meadows rescue cache after a short, three minute flight. She was transported to St. John's Hospital in Jackson by Park ambulance where she was treated for her injuries and released later in the evening.

Analysis
The victim was very fortunate indeed to have escaped practically unscathed from this mishap. Neither person had ever practiced ice axe self-arrest techniques before the incident. Finally, the response time of Ranger Leo Larson, who climbed approximately 5,000 vertical feet in two hours and 15 minutes, is particularly noteworthy. (Source: Renny Jackson, SAR Ranger, Grand Teton National Park)

FALL ON ICY ROCK, WEATHER
Wyoming, Grand Teton National Park, Grand Teton
On July 14, 1992, at 0430, three Exum guides left the lower saddle with seven clients to climb the Exum Ridge on the Grand Teton. The route was in bad condition because of recent new snow and freezing temperatures. The group made good progress, but they were slowed by snow and ice on the route and they were belaying more than usual.

At 0855 one guide (44) was nearing the top of the pitch below the friction pitch when he apparently stepped on some ice and fell. He slid about 50 feet to the bottom of the pitch where his fall was stopped as he collided back first with a large block, breaking eight ribs.

The other two guides administered first aid and then started down with the clients. The guides got the clients down past "the wind tunnel" and then one guide proceeded back to the saddle and called the accident in. He then went back to the accident site with one client.

A difficult short-haul rescue ensued under windy conditions at 1835. The victim was at St. John's Hospital by 1858. The serious injury was further complicated by an infection developed while in the hospital. Recovery was complete, but not for a long time. (Source: From an investigation by Bob Irvine, SAR Ranger, Grand Teton National Park)

(Editor's Note: The guide's fall was due to difficult conditions on a route that is normally no more than a 5.6, and where it is not easy—or usual—to place protection, especially when guiding. This accident is presented because it demonstrates appropriate preparation (clothing) and response by the guides, and another fine rescue carried out by Rangers and the helicopter pilot.)

LOSS OF CONTROL—VOLUNTARY GLISSADE, POOR POSITION
Wyoming, Grand Teton National Park, Disappointment Peak
On July 17, 1992, at 1615, a climber (29) was descending the Lake Ledges route on Disappointment Peak when he fell as he was attempting to glissade down a small patch of

snow and was unable to perform a self-arrest since his ice axe was strapped to his pack at the time. After sliding about 30 to 40 feet, he impacted the rocks below the snow with his left foot. His partner started down and was able to report the accident at the Jenny Lake ranger station at 1750.

The Bridger Teton contract helicopter was requested at 1800 and four rescue team members were assembled for the operation. At 1855 rangers Irvine and Springer were flown to the landing site at Amphitheater Lake. Rangers Kimbrough and Johnson followed a short time later with the remainder of the rescue gear. The victim was evaluated, packaged and carried by litter to the landing site, where he was picked up by helicopter and flown to Lupine Meadows, then transported to hospital. He had fractured his left fibula.

Analysis
This is another example of the most common mechanism of injury in the park's backcountry; that is, a slip on snow—or a deliberate glissade—followed by the inability to stop oneself. (Source: Renny Jackson, SAR Ranger, Grand Teton National Park)

(Editor's Note: There were five such accidents in 1992, not all of which appear in the narrative section. One of them involved a 100 foot slide—voluntary, with no ice axe—that resulted in only a minor injury.)

FALLING ROCK, LOOSE ROCK, FAILURE TO TEST HOLDS
Wyoming, Wind River Range, Seneca Lake
A backpacking and climbing party of eight, all from Minnesota, left the trailhead at the Elkhart Park Guard Station, in the Winds, on July 17, 1992, at 1200. They hiked in approximately six miles and camped at Eklund Lake. On Saturday, Paul Swanson (54), Mary Anderson and Don Schulze left the group and hiked 12 miles to set up base camp for a summit attempt on Gannett Peak. They tried for the summit on Sunday, but were turned back by weather. The weather remained unsettled on Monday and Tuesday. Camp was broken on Tuesday morning, and the three started out to rejoin the rest of the party who had moved up to Seneca Lake and set up camp approximately 11 miles in from the trailhead. Swanson, Anderson and Schulze reached the camp at 1630. Swanson decided to do some boulder/rock scrambling behind camp, followed by Alex Schluender and Anderson. Upon reaching a steeper section of rock, Swanson told Schluender to wait while he checked out the rocks, which might be loose. Climbing up a little, Swanson reached up and a rock, approximately 1.5 feet by six feet, broke loose. Swanson hollered, "Rock," and fell and tumbled about 20 to 30 feet, landing on his chest. Anderson arrived immediately and called for help. The rest of the party in camp below heard the sound of rockfall and Anderson's call for help and arrived within ten minutes.

Swanson was conscious and lying on his stomach. Miller and Schulze took a day pack and started out for the trailhead at 1830, covering the 11 miles and arriving at the van at 2130, drove to Pinedale, and contacted the Sublette County Sheriff at 2200. Miller and Schulze were informed that helicopter flights could not be initiated at night.

Meanwhile, at the accident site, Swanson was insulated from the rock with foam pads and was covered with sleeping bags. He had stated earlier that he had no feeling in his legs and therefore the people with him were afraid to move him due to a possible spinal injury. He lost consciousness and pulse around 2000, and at that point he was turned over and CPR was administered for 20 minutes or so without results. Members of the party took turns staying with him the rest of the night. Temperatures reached the lower 30s.

The victim's body was flown out the next morning. The autopsy revealed skull fractures, massive spinal damage, broken ribs on both sides of the chest, and internal injuries.

Analysis
Paul Swanson was an experienced climber with ascents of Mount Hood, Granite Peak, the Grand and Middle Teton, and the Matterhorn in Switzerland.

Looking back I do not know how to prevent something like this from happening again, other than to stay home. Paul had a feeling that the rock in the area was loose, but I'm sure not a rock of that size, and not the one he was grabbing. The size of the rock probably gave him a false sense of security. It is uncertain whether or not he was hit by the rock that was pulled loose. (Source: From a report submitted by Don Schulze)

STRANDED, OFF ROUTE
Wyoming, Grand Teton National Park, Grand Teton
On July 24, 1993, at 2330, I received a phone call from NPS dispatch. The dispatcher told me that ranger Jim Woodmencey was at the Lower Saddle of the Grand Teton and reported repeatedly seeing the universal distress signal of three light flashes coming from high on the West Face of the Exum Ridge. I talked to Woodmencey by radio and confirmed the report.

It turned out that two climbers (46 and 39) were uninjured and just stuck in the middle of the face. They had become lost on the Exum Ridge route and traversed into the West Face of the Exum and then rappelled 75 feet into nowhere just before dark on June 23.

Additional climbing rangers were flown to the Lower Saddle at 0630 on July 25 and assisted Woodmencey in evacuating them to the Lower Saddle.

During the walk down to the Lower Saddle, one of them was very unsteady on his feet and had to be spotted on easy technical terrain. Ranger Randy Harrington described him as looking like he was going to fall any minute even after Harrington took his pack. This unsteadiness and the fact that both climbers moved very slowly and asked for a belay to rappel off the route led the climbing rangers to discourage them from continuing their proposed plan of climbing the Black Ice Couloir, a much more serious endeavor. Just the approach to the Black Ice is more serious than anything they had climbed.

Another interesting note was that one of them said they were not stuck and that he was shining the light to signal that they were OK. The other disagreed and repeatedly said they were stuck and were signaling that they needed help. (Source: Scott Berkenfield, SAR Ranger, Grand Teton National Park)

STRANDED, CLIMBING ALONE, WEATHER
Wyoming, Grand Teton National Park, Grand Teton
A climber (35) signed out on August 29, 1992, to do a solo climb of the north ridge of the Grand Teton. He discussed the route and his plans extensively with the rangers on duty at the Jenny Lake Ranger Station.

He failed to return as scheduled on the night of the 31st and Ranger Dorward (on routine patrol at the lower saddle) determined that his camp on the Middle Teton Glacier moraine had not been occupied that night, so a search was started on the morning of September 1. Rangers Jackson and Springer went on a recon flight at 1110. They spotted Felber at 1130 on a ledge between the great west chimney and the north ridge, a rope length below the second ledge.

Rangers were flown in three flights to the Lower Saddle. At 1500 they left the Lower Saddle and climbed to the Upper Saddle and out the second ledge to a point 200 feet past the great west chimney. Alexander was then lowered to the victim at 1700. Felber, who was uninjured, was raised with a z-rig to the second ledge while Alexander jumared. They arrived at the second ledge at 1745 and everyone headed back to the Lower Saddle—they arrived there at 2000. Bad weather precluded retrieving the rescue team that evening.

The following morning all seven rangers were flown to Lupine Meadows in two flights in the Yellowstone Lama piloted by Chuck Rogers. A sling load of equipment was also returned from the saddle. All were back by 1225.

Analysis
After returning to the valley, Felber stated that he had started his climb on the 30th as scheduled at 0530 from his camp on the Middle Teton Glacier moraine. He made reasonable progress around the Valhalla Traverse and reached the top of the Grandstand around 1130. From there on up he seemed very confused about the route. He did reach the base of the chockstone pitch, but was unable to climb it. He then climbed the wall to the right and continued straight up to the ledge from which he was eventually rescued. Another rope length of climbing put him on the second ledge just before dark. A short, easy traverse to the south from this point leads to the Upper Saddle.

He spent the night on the second ledge and inexplicably rappelled back down to the ledge below on the morning of the 31st. He remained there until the rescue team fetched him on the afternoon of the 1st. He was unable to climb from the ledge because of the snow that covered the mountain on the nights of the 30th and 31st. (Source: Bob Irvine, SAR Ranger, Grand Teton National Park)

HANDHOLD BROKE OFF, FALL ON ROCK, NO BELAY ANCHORS, NO HARD HATS
Wyoming, Grand Teton National Park, Death Canyon
On September 15, 1992, two experienced climbers (31 and 30) started up the Snaz shortly after noon after registering for their climb that morning at the Jenny Lake Ranger Station. Since both of them had climbed together for many years and had done much longer climbs than the Snaz, it did not seem unreasonable to them to begin at such a late hour. They scrambled up the first pitch unroped and decided not to set up any anchors at the belay for the second pitch. At 1300 as one was leading, he decided to climb out and to the east. (He was about 20 feet off route at that time.) As he attempted to clip his rope into a #3 Camalot that he had placed, his right hand hold broke off and he fell. He was airborne for 40 feet before he landed in a sitting position on the large belay ledge. He rolled another 20 feet down the sloping ledge before coming to rest at the top of the first pitch. He had sustained a serious injury to the left side of his pelvis.

After hearing about the accident by radio, rescue personnel were shuttled to a staging area in Death Canyon by helicopter. Rangers were inserted to a location near the accident scene with medical and climbing equipment. They then climbed to the injured party, made an initial assessment and prepared the patient for transport. He was evacuated from the ledge using the short-haul technique and then flown directly to St. John's Hospital in Jackson. Later in the evening he was flown to Salt Lake City and admitted to the Intensive Care Unit of University Hospital.

Analysis
A variety of modern rescue techniques were used in the evacuation of this critically injured patient including helicopter insertion, technical climbing and short-haul. These techniques, coupled with the application of advanced emergency medical care, are certainly responsible for saving his life. It is interesting to note that although both of these climbers were quite experienced, neither of them was wearing a helmet at the time of the accident nor had they placed any belay anchors. It is very fortunate that the victim managed to prevent his partner from continuing down off the first pitch of the climb. (Source: Renny Jackson, SAR Ranger, Grand Teton National Park)

CORRECTIONS

ANAM 1992, pg. 53, end of second paragraph: The "Source" for the August 4 glassading accident should have read Brian Blair who, in fact, was the victim. Bert Daniels had completed and submitted the accident report, but the "I" referred to was Blair.

TABLE I
REPORTED MOUNTAINEERING ACCIDENTS

	Number of Accidents Reported		Total Persons Involved		Injured		Killed	
	USA	CAN	USA	CAN	USA	CAN	USA	CAN
1951	15		22		11		3	
1952	31		35		17		13	
1953	24		27		12		12	
1954	31		41		31		8	
1955	34		39		28		6	
1956	46		72		54		13	
1957	45		53		28		18	
1958	32		39		23		11	
1959	42	2	56	2	31	0	19	2
1960	47	4	64	12	37	8	19	4
1961	49	9	61	14	45	10	14	4
1962	71	1	90	1	64	0	19	1
1963	68	11	79	12	47	10	19	2
1964	53	11	65	16	44	10	14	3
1965	72	0	90	0	59	0	21	0
1966	67	7	80	9	52	6	16	3
1967	74	10	110	14	63	7	33	5
1968	70	13	87	19	43	12	27	5
1969	94	11	125	17	66	9	29	2
1970	129	11	174	11	88	5	15	5
1971	110	17	138	29	76	11	31	7
1972	141	29	184	42	98	17	49	13
1973	108	6	131	6	85	4	36	2
1974	96	7	177	50	75	1	26	5
1975	78	7	158	22	66	8	19	2
1976	137	16	303	31	210	9	53	6
1977	121	30	277	49	106	21	32	11
1978	118	17	221	19	85	6	42	10
1979	100	36	137	54	83	17	40	19
1980	191	29	295	85	124	26	33	8
1981	97	43	223	119	80	39	39	6
1982	140	48	305	126	120	43	24	14
1983	187	29	442	76	169	26	37	7
1984	182	26	459	63	174	15	26	6
1985	195	27	403	62	190	22	17	3
1986	203	31	406	80	182	25	37	14
1987	192	25	377	79	140	23	32	9
1988	156	18	288	44	155	18	24	4
1989	141	18	272	36	124	11	17	9
1990	136	25	245	50	125	24	24	4
1991	169	20	302	66	147	11	18[1]	6
1992	175	17	351	45	144	11	43	6
Totals	4215	601	7500	1334	3599	475	1037	209

[1] Error last year. Two deaths were reported in Table II for Washington. It should have read eleven (11).

TABLE II

Geographical Districts	1951–1991			1992		
	Number of Accidents	Deaths	Total Persons Involved	Number of Accidents	Deaths	Total Persons Involved
Canada						
Alberta	276	81	614	9	4	17
British Columbia	234	90	522	5	2	15
Yukon Territory	29	25	63	2	0	9
Ontario	27	6	50	0	0	0
Quebec	21	5	49	1	0	4
East Arctic	7	2	20	0	0	0
West Arctic	1	1	2	0	0	0
Practice Cliffs[1]	13	2	18	0	0	0
United States						
Alaska	290	111	873	16	15	45
Arizona, Nevada Texas	47	5	81	4	1	10
Atlantic–North	547	82	859	29	4	57
Atlantic–South	39	10	66	6	1	11
California	791	211	1686	41	4	76
Central	82	7	138	1	1	1
Colorado/Oklahoma	518	161	866	12	7	29
Montana, Idaho South Dakota	49	22	73	6	0	12
Oregon	95	51	238	7	1	14
Utah, New Mexico	94	32	165	2	0	4
Washington	801	246[2]	1392	32	8	57
Wyoming	381	81	677	19	1	35
Artificial Walls	2	0	2	0	0	0

[1]This category includes bouldering, as well as artificial climbing walls, buildings, and so forth. These are also added to the count of each state and province, but not to the total count, though that error has been made in previous years.

[2]This figure reflects an addition of nine (9) to last year's total, to correct an error in recording only two (2) deaths for this state.

(Editor's Note: The Practice Cliffs category has been removed from the U.S. data and replaced with Artificial Walls.)

TABLE III

	1951–91 USA	1959–91 CAN.	1992 USA	1992 CAN.
Terrain				
Rock	2925	354	120	7
Snow	1835	277	44	3
Ice	151	62	11	7
River	12	3	0	0
Unknown	22	6	0	0
Ascent or Descent				
Ascent	2634	365	125	12
Descent	1652	252	49	5
Unknown	241	1	1	0
Immediate Cause				
Fall or slip on rock	1896	183	92	3
Slip on snow or ice	668	134	24	4
Falling rock or object	410	101	13	1
Exceeding abilities	324	27	16	0
Avalanche	237	94	6	1
Exposure	211	12	3	0
Illness[1]	201	17	12	0
Stranded	188	39	13	2
Rappel Falure/Error	154	22	5	2
Loss of control/voluntary glissade	149	13	5	1
Fall into crevasse/moat	113	34	5	2
Failure to follow route	96	18	5	0
Piton pulled out	69	12	1	0
Nut/chock pulled out	56	3	9	0
Faulty use of crampons	51	4	0	1
Lightning	37	6	2	0
Skiing	37	9	3	0
Ascending too fast	33	0	0	0
Equipment failure	5	2	0	0
Other[2]	101	13	15	1
Unknown	48	8	1	0
Contributory Causes				
Climbing unroped	807	125	15	5
Exceeding abilities	771	142	14	2
Inadequate equipment	477	60	13	3
Weather	308	35	18	3
Placed no/inadequate protection	343	39	34	2
Climbing alone	278	48	6	2
No hard hat	166	18	12	1
Nut/chock pulled out	141	12	7	0
Darkness	100	12	2	1
Piton pulled out	79	10	2	0
Party separated	85	15	4	0

	1951–91 USA	1959–91 CAN.	1992 USA	1992 CAN.
Contributory Causes (cont.)				
Poor position	73	9	11	1
Failure to test holds	58	14	3	0
Exposure	52	9	0	0
Inadequate belay	56	5	11	4
Failed to follow directions	49	3	0	2
Illness[1]	27	4	0	0
Equipment failure	8	3	0	1
Other[2]	184	49	6	14
Age of Individuals				
Under 15	99	11	7	0
15-20	1065	192	11	1
21-25	1258	216	37	1
26-30	842	172	39	4
31-35	482	82	32	3
36-50	614	92	59	1
Over 50	91	12	5	2
Unknown	719	321	32	33
Experience Level				
None/Little	1347	252	25	4
Moderate (1 to 3 years)	1218	284	20	21
Experienced	1071	295	58	16
Unknown	1125	210	99	4
Month of Year				
January	151	9	8	0
February	155	31	8	1
March	214	35	4	1
April	281	25	7	2
May	572	37	33	1
June	701	41	32	1
July	802	192	30	4
August	704	199	26	3
September	979	39	12	3
October	271	29	12	0
November	138	4	2	1
December	53	16	1	0
Type of Injury/Illness (Data since 1984)				
Fracture	546	69	82	9
Laceration	234	26	32	3
Abrasion	145	19	20	3
Bruise	147	22	21	5
Sprain/strain	130	12	14	0
Concussion	68	7	9	3
Frostbite	57	4	9	0
Hypothermia	49	7	9	0

	1951–91 USA	1959–91 CAN.	1992 USA	1992 CAN.
Type of Injury/Illness (cont.)				
Dislocation	34	5	9	0
Puncture	19	2	1	0
HAPE	34	0	6	0
Acute Mountain Sickness	11	0	0	0
CE	5	0	1	0
Other[1]	118	20	7	1
None	34	3	15	0

[1]These include: a) flail chest; b) pneumothorax (2); c) atrial fibrillation; d) severe dehydration; e) fatigue (3); f) infection; g) renal failure; h) snow blindness; i) pre-existing conditions (e.g., knee spontaneously dislocates); j) cardiac arrest; and k) ear detached.

[2]These include: a) belay rope end went through belay device while lowering; b) rappel brake system inadequate; c) failure to clip into both loops of an anchor sling; d) belay anchor system came away; e) 9mm poly pro fixed rope, used to rappel on, broke; f) rope frayed through—rubbed on edge while jumarring (also "inadequate protection"); g) pulled various size rocks off, causing falls and crushing injuries (3); h) knots "came undone" (3); i) harness "came undone"; j) patella spontaneously dislocated causing a fall; k) rappel ropes froze; l) ascenders "detached" from rope; m) miscommunication (4); n) not understanding ice conditions, i.e., history of snow/ice formations (2); o) late start (lightning in afternoon); p) euphoria—beautiful weather, ideal ski condition—but in avalance terrain.

MOUNTAIN RESCUE ASSOCIATION OFFICERS

Kevin Walker, *President*
1408 Mountain Avenue
San Jacinto, CA 92583

Tim Cochrane, *Vice President*
PO Box 115
Vail, CO 81658

Dick Sale, *Secretary/Treasurer*
5286 Townsend Avenue
Eagle Rock, CA 90041

Tim Kovacs, *Member at large*
PO Box 4004
Phoenix, AZ 85030-4004

Rocky Henderson, *Member at large*
12480 S.E. Wiese
Boring, OR 97009

MOUNTAIN RESCUE ASSOCIATION, INC.
200 Union Boulevard, Suite 430-1355
Denver, CO 80220

MOUNTAIN RESCUE GROUPS IN NORTH AMERICA
(Where not obvious, area covered is indicated in parentheses)
°Indicates membership in Mountain Rescue Association

ALASKA
Alaska Mountain Rescue Group,° PO Box 241102, Anchorage, AK 99524
U. S. Army Northern Warfare Training Center,° Fort Greeley, AK, APO Seattle 98733
Denali National Park Ranger Station, Talkeetna, AK 99676

ALBERTA
Banff Park Warden Service, Banff National Park, PO Box 900, Banff, Alberta T0L 0C0
Jasper Park Warden Service, Jasper National Park, PO Box 10, Jasper, Alberta T0E 1E0
Kananaskis Park Warden Service, Kananaskis Provincial Park, General Delivery, Seebe,
    Alberta T0L 1X0 (Alberta outside National Parks)
Waterton Park Warden Service, Waterton National Park, Waterton, Alberta T0K 2M0

ARIZONA
Arizona Mountaineering Club Rescue Team, PO Box 1695, Phoenix, AZ 85030
Central Arizona Mountain Rescue Association,° PO Box 4004, Phoenix, AZ 85030
Grand Canyon National Park Rescue Team,° PO Box 129, Grand Canyon, AZ 86023
Southern Arizona Rescue Association, Inc.,° PO Box 12892, Tucson, AZ 85732
Sedona Fire Dept./Technical Rescue Group, PO Box 3964, West Sedona, AZ 86340

BRITISH COLUMBIA
Columbia Mountain Rescue Group, Royal Canadian Mounted Police, Invermere,
B.C. V0A 1K0 (East Kootenays)
Glacier Revelstoke Park Warden Service, Glacier Revelstoke National Park, PO Box 350,
    Revelstoke, B.C. V0E 2S0)
Kootenay Park Warden Service, Kootenay National Park, PO Box 220, Radium Hot
    Springs, B.C. V0A 1M0
Mountain Rescue Group, c/o Frank Baumann, PO Box 1846, Squamish, B.C. V0N 3G0
    (Coast Range, Northern Cascades)
North Shore Rescue Team,° 165 East 13th Street, North Vancouver, B.C. V7L 2L3

CALIFORNIA
Altadena Mountain Rescue Team, Inc.,° 780 E. Altadena Drive, Altadena, CA 91001
    (Los Angeles County)
Bay Area Mountain Rescue Unit, Inc.,° PO Box 6384, Stanford, CA 94309 (Northern
    Sierra Nevada)
China Lake Mountain Rescue Group,° PO Box 2037, Ridgecrest, CA 93555 (Southern
    Sierra Nevada)
De Anza Rescue Unit, PO Box 1599, El Centro, CA 92243 (Imperial Valley, Baja)
Inyo County Sheriff's Posse,° PO Box 982, Bishop, CA 93514
Joshua Tree National Monument SAR,° 74485 National Monument Dr., Twenty-nine
    Palms, CA 92277
June Lake Mountain Rescue Team,° P. O. Box 436, June Lake, CA 93529

Los Padres Search and Rescue Team,° PO Box 30400, Santa Barbara, CA 93130
Malibu Mountain Rescue Team,° PO Box 222, Malibu, CA 90265
Montrose Search and Rescue Team,° PO Box 404, Montrose, CA 91021 (Los Angeles County)
Riverside Mountain Rescue Unit,° PO Box 5444, Riverside, CA 92517 (Riverside County)
Saddleback Search & Rescue Team, PO Box 5222, Orange, CA 92667
San Diego Mountain Rescue Team,° PO Box 81602, San Diego, CA 92138
San Dimas Mountain Rescue Team,° PO Box 35, San Dimas, CA 91733
San Gorgonio Search & Rescue Team, San Bernardino Sheriff, San Bernardino, CA 92400 (San Bernardino Mountains)
Santa Clarita Valley Search and Rescue,° 23740 Magic Mountain Parkway, Valencia, CA 91355
Sequoia-Kings Canyon National Park Rescue Team,° Three Rivers, CA 93271
Sierra Madre Search and Rescue Team,° PO Box 24, Sierra Madre, CA 91025 (Southwestern United States, Baja, California)
Yosemite National Park Rescue Team, Inc.° PO Box 577, Yosemite National Park, CA 95389

COLORADO
Alpine Rescue Team, Inc.° PO Box 934, Evergreen, CO 80439 (Front Range)
Colorado Ground Search and Rescue,° 2391 S. Ash Street, Denver, CO 80222
El Paso County Search & Rescue, Inc.,° PO Box 9922, Manitou Springs, CO 80932
Eldorado Canyon State Park,° PO Box B, Eldorado Springs, CO 80025
Garfield Search & Rescue,° PO Box 1116, Glenwood Springs, CO 81602
Grand County Search & Rescue,° PO Box 172, Winter Park, CO 80482
Larimer County Search & Rescue,° PO Box 1271, Fort Collins, CO 80522
Mountain Rescue—Aspen, Inc.° PO Box 4446, Aspen, CO 81612 (Western Slope)
Ouray Mountain Rescue Team, PO Box 220, Ouray, CO 81427 (Gunnison National Park, Rio Grande National Forest, Uncompahgre Park)
Rocky Mountain National Park Rescue Team,° Estes Park, CO 80517
Rocky Mountain Rescue Group, Inc.,° PO Box Y, Boulder, CO 80306
San Juan Mountain SAR, PO Box 4, Silverton, CO 81433
Summit County Rescue Group,° PO Box 1794, Breckenridge, CO 80424
Vail Mountain Rescue Group,° PO Box 115, Vail, CO 81658
Western State Mountain Rescue Team,° Western State College, Gunnison, CO 81231

IDAHO
Idaho Mountain Search and Rescue,° PO Box 8714, Boise, ID 83707
Palouse-Clearwater Search and Rescue,° Route 1, Box 103-B, Troy, ID 83871

MAINE
Baxter State Park Mountain Rescue Team,° 64 Balsam Drive, Millinocket, ME 04462

MONTANA
Glacier National Park Rescue Service,° PO Box 636, Essex, MT 59916
Lewis and Clark Search and Rescue,° PO Box 473, Helena, MT 59601

NEW HAMPSHIRE
Appalachian Mountain Club, Pinkham Notch Camp, Gorham, NH 03581 (White Mountains)
Mountain Rescue Service,° PO Box 494, North Conway, NH 03860

NEW MEXICO
Albuquerque Mountain Rescue Council,° PO Box 53396, Albuquerque, NM 87153
St. John's College Search and Rescue Team, PO Box 350, St. John's College, Camino de
    Cruz Blanca, Santa Fee, NM 87501 (Northern New Mexico, Southern Colorado)

NORTHWEST TERRITORIES
Auyuittuq Park Warden Service, Auyuittuq National Park, Pangnirtung, N.W.T. X0A 0R0

OREGON
Alpinees, Inc.,° 3571 Belmont Dr., Hood River, OR 97301 (Hood River County)
Corvallis Mountain Rescue Unit,° PO Box 116, Corvallis, OR 97339 (Central Cascades)
Crater Lake National Park Rescue Team, PO Box 7, Crater Lake, OR 97604
Eugene Mountain Rescue,° PO Box 10081, Eugene, OR 97401 (Oregon Cascades)
Hood River Crag Rates,° 1450 Nunamaker, Salem, OR 97031
Portland Mountain Rescue,° PO Box 1222, Portland, OR 97207

UTAH
American Search Dogs,° 4939 Benlomand, Ogden, UT 84003
Rocky Mountain Rescue Dogs,° 9624 S. 1210 E., Sandy, UT 84070
Salt Lake County Sheriff Search and Rescue,° 2942 Cardiff Road, Salt Lake City, UT 84121
Zion National Park°, Chief Ranger, Springdale, UT 84767

VERMONT
Mountain Cold Weather Rescue Team, Norwich University, Northfield, VT 05663

VIRGINIA
Appalachian Search and Rescue Conference°, PO Box 430, Flint Hill, VA 22627 (Blue
    Ridge and Shenandoah Mountains and Southwest Virginia)

WASHINGTON
Bellingham Mountain Rescue Council°, PO Box 292, Bellingham, WA 98225 (Whatcom
    County)
Central Washington Mountain Rescue Council°, PO Box 2663, Yakima, WA 98907
    (Washington)
Everett Mountain Rescue Unit°, PO Box 2566, Everett, WA 98203 (North Central
    Cascades)
Mount Rainier National Park Rescue Team°, Longmire, WA 98397 (Mount Rainier
    National Park)
Mountain Rescue Council, Inc., PO Box 67, Seattle, WA 98111 (Washington)
North Cascades National Park Rescue Team°, 2105 Highway 20, Sedro Woolley,
    WA 98284

Olympic Mountain Rescue°, PO Box 4244, Bremerton, WA 98312 (Olympic Range, Cascades)

Olympic National Park Rescue Team°, 600 Park Ave., Port Angeles, WA 98362 (Olympic National Park)

Skagit Mountain Rescue Unit°, 128 4th St., Mount Vernon, WA 98273 (Northern Cascades)

Tacoma Mountain Rescue Unit°, 7910 "A" St., Tacoma, WA 98408 (Central Washington, Cascades, Olympics)

WYOMING

Grand Teton National Park Mountain Search and Rescue Team°, PO Box 67, Moose, WY 83012 (Grand Teton National Park)

Mountain Rescue Outing Club, University of Wyoming, Laramie, WY 82071 (Wyoming)

YUKON

Kluane Park Warden Service, Kluane National Park, Haines Junction, Yukon Y0B 1L0